*Happy birthday 1980 - August 12, 13, and 14
France. England.
All my love, with appropriate herbs.
Peter.*

herb growing

herb gro

SAMPSON LOW

wing

a visual guide
by the DIAGRAM GROUP

First published in 1978 by
Sampson Low, Berkshire House,
Queen Street, Maidenhead,
Berkshire SL6 1NF

© Diagram Visual Information Ltd
All rights reserved
Printed by Purnell & Sons Ltd

ISBN 562 00103 4

The Diagram Group

Editor	Bernard Cleves
Assistant Editor	Maureen Cartwright
Art Director	Kathleen McDougall
Artists	Stephen Clark, Robert Galvin, Brian Hewson, Richard Hummerstone, Susan Kinsey, Pavel Kostal, Janos Marffy, Graham Rosewarne
Consultants	J. J. Wells, M.P., Wells & Winter Ltd (nurserymen), Mereworth, Maidstone, Kent. J. & B. Hugo, Ashfields Nursery, Hinstock, Market Drayton, Salop.
Picture credits	The Mansell Collection

foreword

What is a herb? The dictionary has two different definitions that to some extent contradict each other. One says that a herb is a plant whose stem does not become woody and persistent, but dies down to ground level after flowering. The other says that the word is applied to a plant whose leaves, or stem or flowers, are used for food or medicine, or for their scent or flavour.

If not from their own gardening experience, most people could name a few of the commonly used herbs from the racks of herbs and spices displayed in the grocer's shop. Mint, parsley and thyme come to mind at once; many people, if they scratched their heads, could perhaps think up a few more, such as fennel, tarragon and basil. But there are many more, and this book tells you about over 50 cultivated herbs and nearly a score of wild ones that may play a part in your life occasionally, whether you know it or not. Herbs are used to give a subtle taste to liqueurs, some of which contain a number of different ones. And they are also used to mask otherwise unpleasant flavours in medicines.

But most people do not grow herbs to flavour liqueurs or medicines. They grow them mainly for use in cooking, or to include their fragrance in toilet preparations, pot-pourri, sachets and the like. So this book serves two purposes: it tells you how to grow and recognize herbs; and it gives ideas for using them in the home. At the same time it contains useful and interesting information about their other uses.

Today, more and more people seem to be returning to the use of fresh and dried herbs in cooking, probably because modern methods of preservation tend to destroy the original taste of the food. And in addition, many people are turning to growing their own herbs, for freshness and cheapness. This book will tell you all about herbs, what they look like and how to cultivate them. It tells you also how to recognize some of the more useful wild herbs that you may come across in your wanderings. And finally it suggests some of the uses you can make of the harvest from your herb garden. You will soon discover many more for yourself.

contents

8 **Chapter one:**
  Growing herbs
10 Introduction to growing
12 Growing outdoors
14 Growing indoors
16 Making a start
18 Growing from seed
20 More plants
22 Repotting

24 **Chapter two:**
  Cultivated herbs
26 Naming herbs
30 Arrangement of chapter
32 Agrimony
33 Garlic
34 Chives
35 Dill
36 Angelica
37 Camomile
38 Chervil
39 Tarragon
40 Borage
42 Pot marigold
43 Caraway
44 Parsley
45 Chicory
46 Horseradish
47 Coriander
48 Saffron
49 Cumin
50 Finocchio
51 Fennel
52 Wintergreen
53 Hyssop
54 Elecampane
56 Juniper
57 Bay
58 Lavender
60 Lovage

61 Lemon verbena
62 White horehound
63 Lemon balm
64 Mints
66 Bergamot
67 Sweet cicely
68 Myrtle
69 Basil
70 Marjorams
72 Anise
73 Purslane
74 Rose
75 Rosemary
76 Sorrel
77 Rue
78 Sage
79 Elder
80 Salad burnet
81 Savory
82 Comfrey
84 Tansy
85 Costmary
86 Thyme
87 Nasturtium
88 Valerian
89 Corn salad
90 Mullein
92 Violet

94 **Chapter three:** **Wild herbs**	118 **Chapter four:** **How to use herbs**
96 Naming herbs	120 Introduction to using herbs
97 Arrangement of chapter	
98 Where they grow	122 Drying herbs
100 Lady's mantle	124 Herbs in the kitchen
101 Burdock	130 The most useful herbs
102 Wormwood	132 Home-made wines
103 Mugwort	134 Herb teas
104 Woodruff	136 Fragrances
105 Deadly nightshade	138 Fragrant keepsakes
106 Foxglove	140 Sweets
107 Willow-herb	142 **Index**
108 Witch hazel	
109 Henbane	
110 Popppy	
112 Cowslip	
113 Chickweed	
114 Meadowsweet	
115 Betony	
116 Dandelion	
117 Nettle	

chapter one
growing herbs

This French chateau had a herb garden in the courtyard.

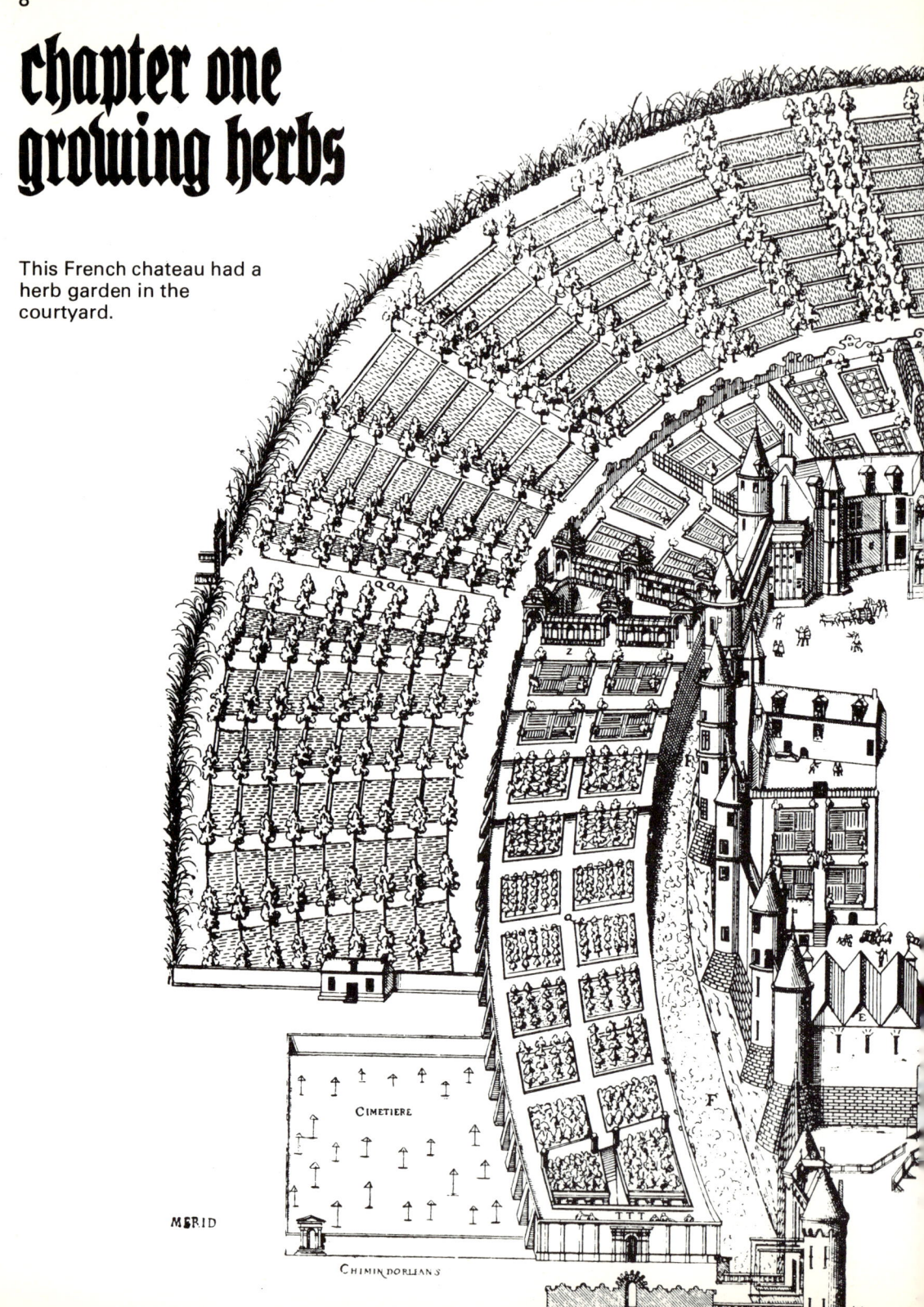

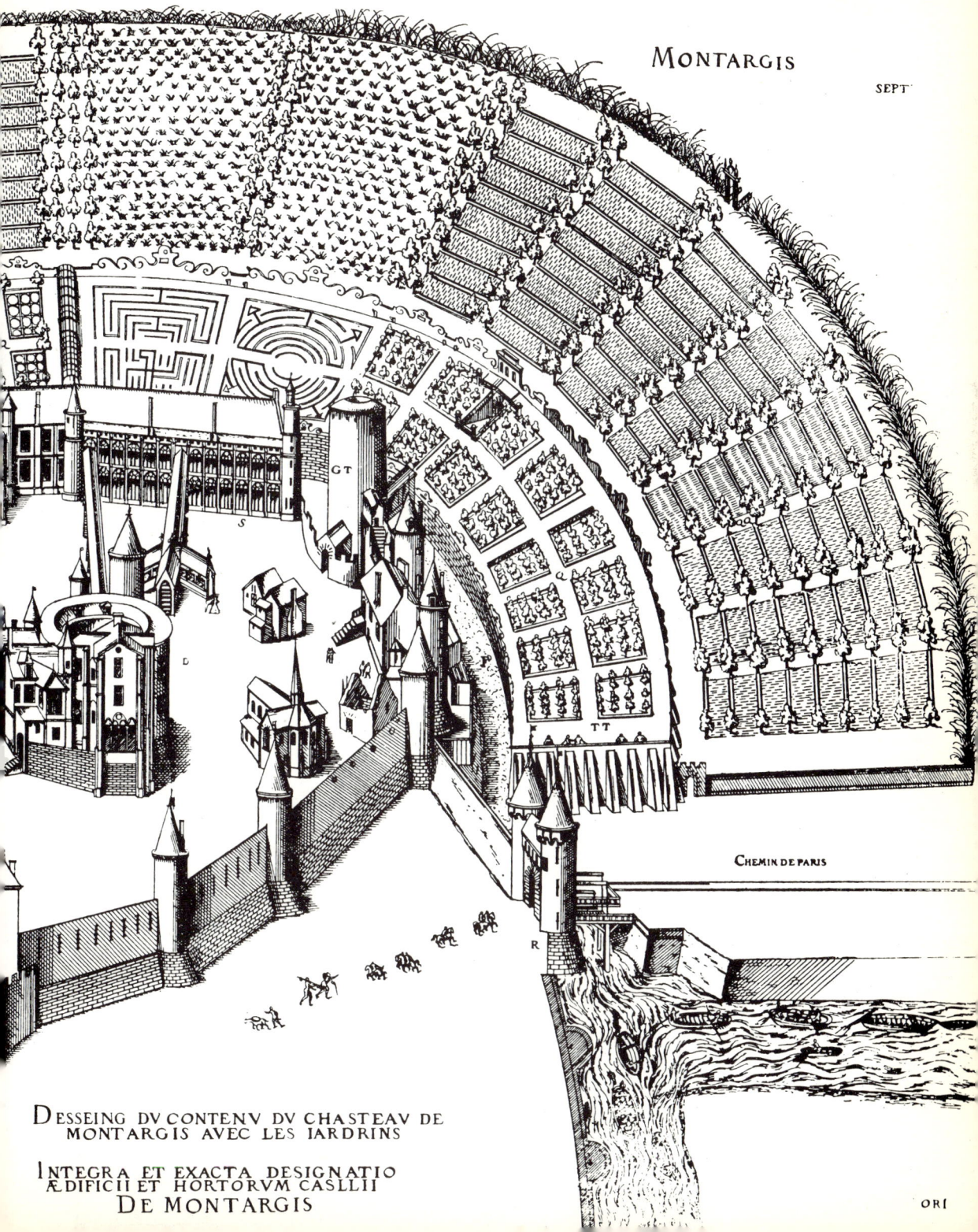

Desseing dv contenv dv chasteav de Montargis avec les iardrins

Integra et exacta designatio ædificii et hortorvm caslii de Montargis

introduction to growing

Herbs are not difficult to grow, nor do they make great demands on the gardener's time and labour once they are established. Among other things this chapter tells you how you can start off a modest herb garden of your own, and how, if you can't do that, you can grow herbs on the patio, backyard or balcony, or even inside the house.

There are a few basic principles that need to be kept in mind. Most herbs like the sun and dislike too much wind. Also they dislike wet roots, which means that the soil in which you choose to grow them should be well drained; a little sand around the roots helps when planting.

Herbs are not very demanding as to soil, so long as it is not wet and clayey. A regular application of well-rotted compost each year will probably be enough, for it may well be that if the plant puts on excessive growth some of the flavour and aroma of its foliage will be lost.

Herbs are either annuals or perennials: the former, of course, die at the end of the year, whereas the latter continue for at least a few years. This means that parts of your herb garden will be alive all the time, but other parts will be bare until sown or planted up again. This should be borne in mind when planning your garden, and incidentally gives you the chance to ring the changes on your herb pattern every spring.

Although the parts of your herb garden occupied by perennials may be 'alive' during the winter, they may very well not appear to be

so. This is because most perennials die down to the ground, leaving only the roots still living beneath the surface with no visible sign of life above. They will grow again next spring or summer, so don't start digging up the garden because nothing shows on the surface. Much better is to keep a careful record or mark where your perennials are. Some annuals are self-seeding and thus perpetuate themselves: borage is a good example. There are many reliable growers of herbs throughout the country who will supply seeds or plants by post.

One advantage that herbs have over vegetables – and for that matter over many flowers – for the owner of the small garden, is that they take up so much less room. To grow lettuces for a family throughout the summer and autumn you need to have one or two longish rows growing at the same time. Cabbages and sprouts, grown as they should be up to 2 ft (60 cm) apart, take up a big slice of the vegetable plot. But unless you are growing commercially you don't need more than a couple of plants of most herbs. One rosemary bush tucked in a corner will supply all your needs of that fragrant herb; a small bay tree in a tub and one or two sage bushes are more than enough. Even mint and parsley can be kept confined to small areas.

With most herbs the best time to gather leaves, whether to use fresh in the kitchen or dried for winter, or for pot-pourri or sachets, is just before flowering time. It is then that the leaves have their finest flavour and fragrance.

12 Chapter one

growing outdoors

Many of our most common herbs were originally natives of the Mediterranean area, which is probably why most of them like an open, sunny, well-drained position and dislike a heavy clay soil in which to grow.

In the great houses, herbs were traditionally grown in very formal gardens set aside for the purpose, with separate beds divided by paving, and often with a small pool. Nothing could be more attractive if you have the space, but as this is unlikely it is best to think in terms of either growing your herbs in borders or setting aside a less ambitious section of the garden. The actual cultivation of the herbs will be the same wherever you grow them.

You must remember that many herbs have small flowers and do not grow very tall, so thought must be given to placing them where they can be seen and smelled to best advantage. And bear in mind that if you are growing herbs for regular culinary use it is wise to plant the ones most often used where they can be easily gathered.

Only a small space is needed to grow the most commonly used herbs. The plot should be sheltered from the wind. Herbs do not demand a rich soil, but they do need good drainage and careful soil preparation. It is important that the beds should be kept well weeded, but otherwise the plants need little actual cultivation. A simple herb garden can be made in a small plot about 10 ft (3 m) square, with paths along the diagonals and a circle in the centre. Paths need be only 18 in (45 cm) wide, and the centre circle whatever size you like, leaving four roughly triangular beds. The paths can be paved with bricks or small concrete slabs, to provide easy access.

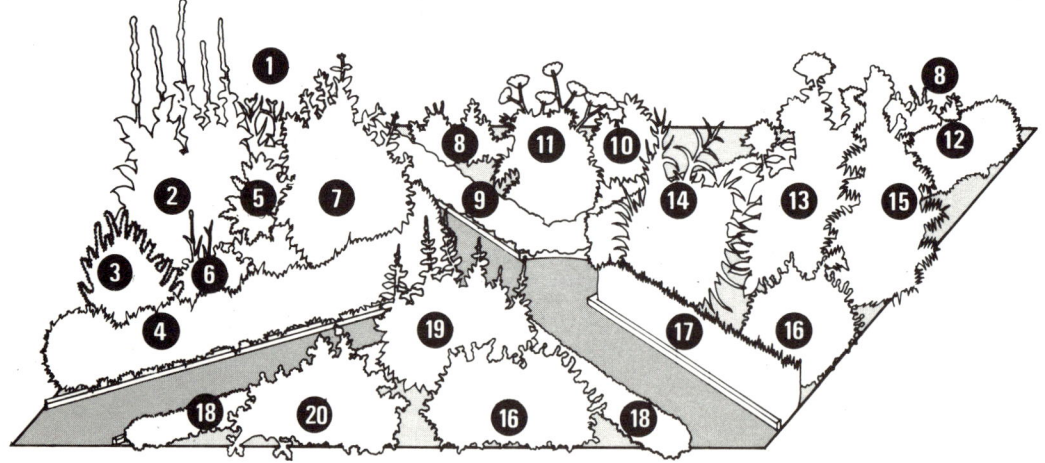

Growing herbs 13

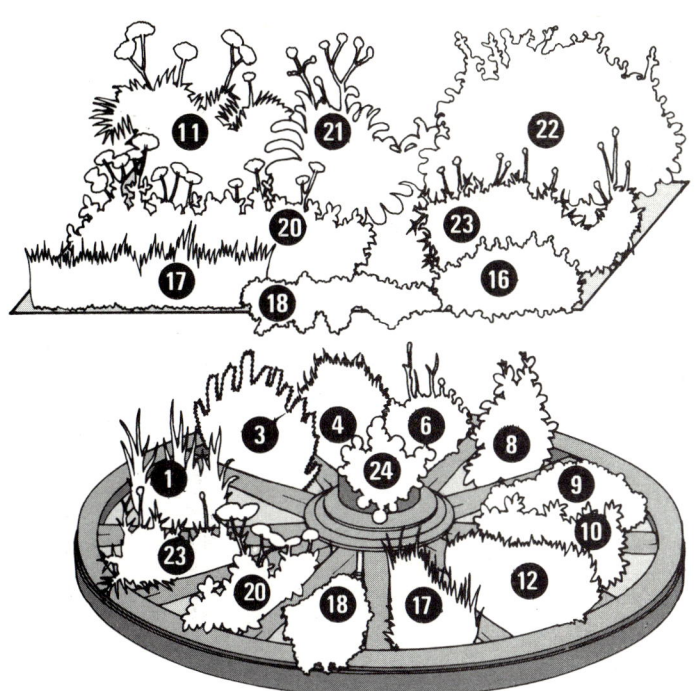

Herbs can contribute to a colourful border while being useful. Low-growing chervil, chives and pot marjoram provide attractive splashes of white, mauve and rose pink at the front of the mixed flower border. Fennel looks well among tall plants at the back of the border, with its fine golden-yellow flowers and blue-green leaves.

An old and charming idea is to use a wooden cartwheel as the basis of a herb garden, growing the herbs in the spaces between the spokes. To prevent the wheel rotting quickly, the wood should be raised above the soil level on stones or concrete. To keep the wheel looking attractive, give it an occasional lick of paint and trim the herbs.

1 garlic
2 mullein
3 rosemary
4 lavender
5 sweet cicely
6 salad burnet
7 lemon balm
8 mint
9 parsley
10 sage
11 fennel
12 hyssop
13 bergamot
14 tarragon
15 tansy
16 marjoram
17 chives
18 thyme
19 basil
20 chervil
21 chicory
22 borage
23 camomile
24 nasturtium

If you cannot spare the space for a plot devoted entirely to herbs, don't forget that there are two other ways of growing them. One (see pages 14–15) is to grow them indoors or on the patio. The other is to spread them around in the flower and vegetable plots, among your other plants. It cannot be over-stressed that many herbs are not only useful but also very decorative, and will amply repay your hospitality. Lavender makes a delightful and colourful border in any part of the garden. But the various kinds of thyme, pot marjoram, chives and hyssop are also ornamental and look well among flowers. Even common parsley looks surprisingly decorative planted in the spaces among the rose bushes.

If you have the awkward misfortune to have a very heavy soil in your garden, it is advisable to plant or divide your herbs in the spring. A little sand in the bottom of each hole when planting will help to improve the drainage.

> ... I have oft heard
> My mother Circe with the
>   Sirens three,
> Culling their potent
>   herbs and baleful drugs.
> Milton (1608–74) –
> *Comus*

Chapter one

growing indoors

Do not despair of growing enough herbs for the kitchen if you have no garden, or if there is no space to spare in the garden for herbs. There are many herbs that are quite suitable for growing in window-boxes, on the patio or the doorstep, in a corner of the balcony if you are a flat-dweller, or indeed inside the house itself, in pots or hanging baskets. Herbs are very accommodating, and provided you give them a modest corner and a minimum of care, they will repay you many times.

Although the kitchen might seem to be the obvious place in which to grow herbs indoors, because they would be so handy for instant use, this is not a very good idea. The kitchen is always more subject to changes of temperature and atmosphere than the other rooms of the house. The room gets very hot while you are cooking, and then you fling open a window and the cold fresh air rushes in, right past the poor plant. On the whole, herbs are plants of very regular habits. Indeed, very few plants can cope with wide changes of temperature, although some hardy ones tolerate such conditions. A small lobby exposed to the sun's rays would be a better place, but almost any convenient sunny windowsill in the house can be used.

Nevertheless many people do manage to grow herbs in their kitchen with modest success, especially if there is plenty of natural light. Chives, mint and parsley can be grown in pots on the windowsill, and look and smell very fresh. Mint is also very useful in the kitchen because it deters flies.

An ordinary hanging basket can be used in a sunny window to grow a plentiful supply of parsley for use in the kitchen. But you must remember that parsley is a plant that takes a long time to germinate; there may be a long wait after you have planted the seeds, so don't lose patience and throw it out before it has even begun to grow!

The decorative terracotta jars with holes in the sides are excellent for growing a small supply of herbs if you have the space. They look nice, and provide a selection of herbs ready to pick when needed. The jar is filled with soil, and seedlings are pushed into the holes and the top. Turn the jar from time to time.

Growing herbs 15

Window-boxes are a good idea if your window ledges are big enough to take one. They need a depth of soil of not less than 9 in (23 cm). You should be able to grow most of the smaller herbs in a window-box, but the shallowness of the soil and the exposure to wind and weather will probably exhaust the soil more quickly than in the open garden. So it is a good idea to change the soil in the window-box once a year, and to include plenty of peat and compost; and drainage is very important. If you cannot have a window-box, perhaps you can put a box on a balcony if you live in a flat. If the soil is about 9 in (23 cm) deep, the other dimensions of the box can be adjusted to fit the available space.

If you have a pleasant sun-bathed patio, you can probably grow your herbs in the most convenient place, beside the kitchen door. Herbs are usually quite shallow-rooted, and they therefore grow very well in pots and containers of all kinds. For an average family you will not need vast quantities of herbs, but just a sprig of two at a time, so 1 plant of each variety is usually enough. Perhaps the most decorative of the herbs you can grow on a patio is the bay tree. Normally this can grow to a height of 25 ft (7.6 m), but planted in an ornamental tub it can be kept down to a few feet, and shaped so that its shiny evergreen leaves show up well against the wall, as well as providing a ready supply for the cook.

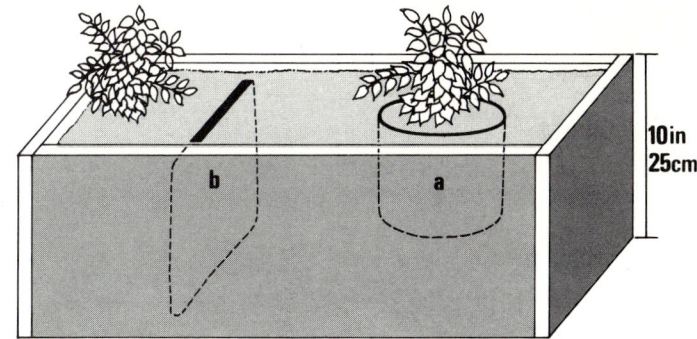

When you grow mint, the greatest problem is always to stop it spreading! In a window-box you can either use a sunken metal container as you would in a garden – an empty bottomless tin can (**a**) will be adequate – or use a piece of slate or an old tile (**b**) across the box to keep the mint roots from spreading horizontally along the window-box.

Among the herbs that combine business and pleasure, as it were, by both looking attractive in pots or window-boxes and being very useful in the kitchen, are rosemary, sage, tarragon and thyme. Rosemary needs a fairly large pot or container. Savory and basil also have shallow roots and do well in window-boxes.

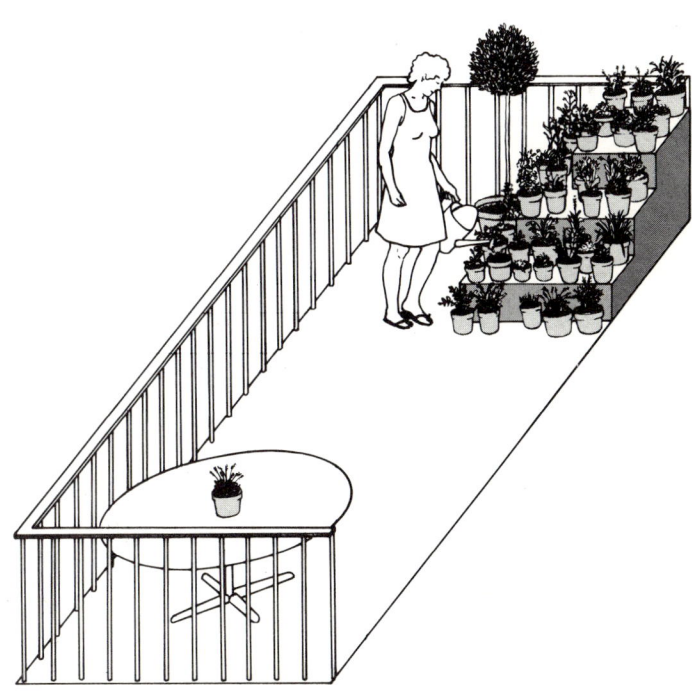

16 Chapter one

making a start

The great majority of herbs can be grown from seed, but sometimes it is a lot easier to grow from root cuttings or divisions, or even by layering. With a few of the larger herbs, if you need only a single tree or shrub, it is simpler to buy the plant from a reputable nurseryman; this is the case with a bay tree, for instance, or a juniper bush. If you have a kind friend or neighbour, you may be able to persuade him to give you cuttings or root divisions, perhaps giving him some of yours in return. And by taking cuttings and dividing the larger clumps of your own plants, you can add to your stock or replace older plants with new ones. But by far the cheapest and most absorbing way to acquire new herbs (in the absence of kind friends) is to grow them from seed.

If you are going to grow herbs in the garden,

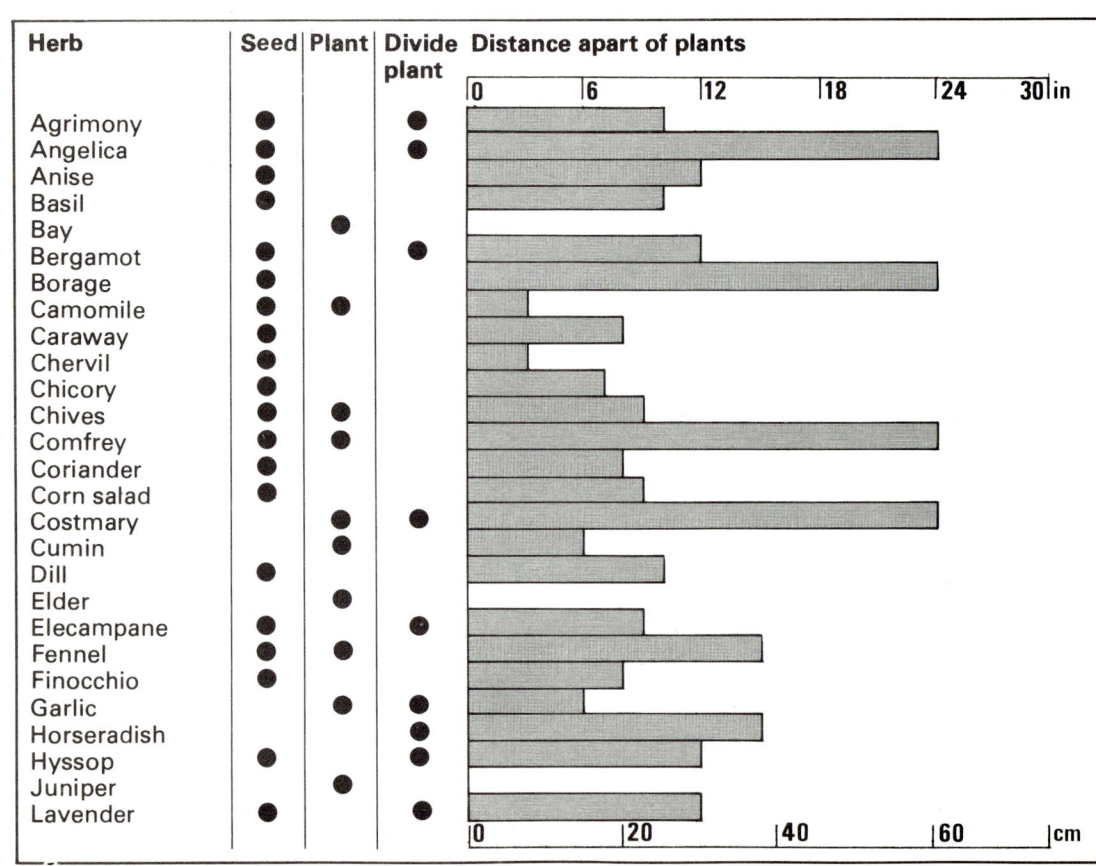

Growing herbs 17

the ideal soil is fairly light and extremely well-drained. Most herbs prefer a neutral or slightly alkaline soil, but a few (angelica, for example) prefer the soil to be slightly acid. If the herb garden has a very acid soil you must give it a regular dressing of lime.

The area you choose for your herb garden should also get quite a lot of sunshine, as most herbs like to bask in the sun; but camomile and mint prefer to have some shade too.

There is no single piece of advice that will cover the time of year to plant all your herbs, because they differ in their individual requirements: if you turn to Chapter 2, you will find that the planting times are given for each separate herb. But whenever and whatever you are planting, try to choose a day when the soil is fairly damp but not soaking wet.

A few items have been left out of the table below. Elder, juniper and bay are commonly grown singly for herbal uses, so the question of spacing them out does not arise.

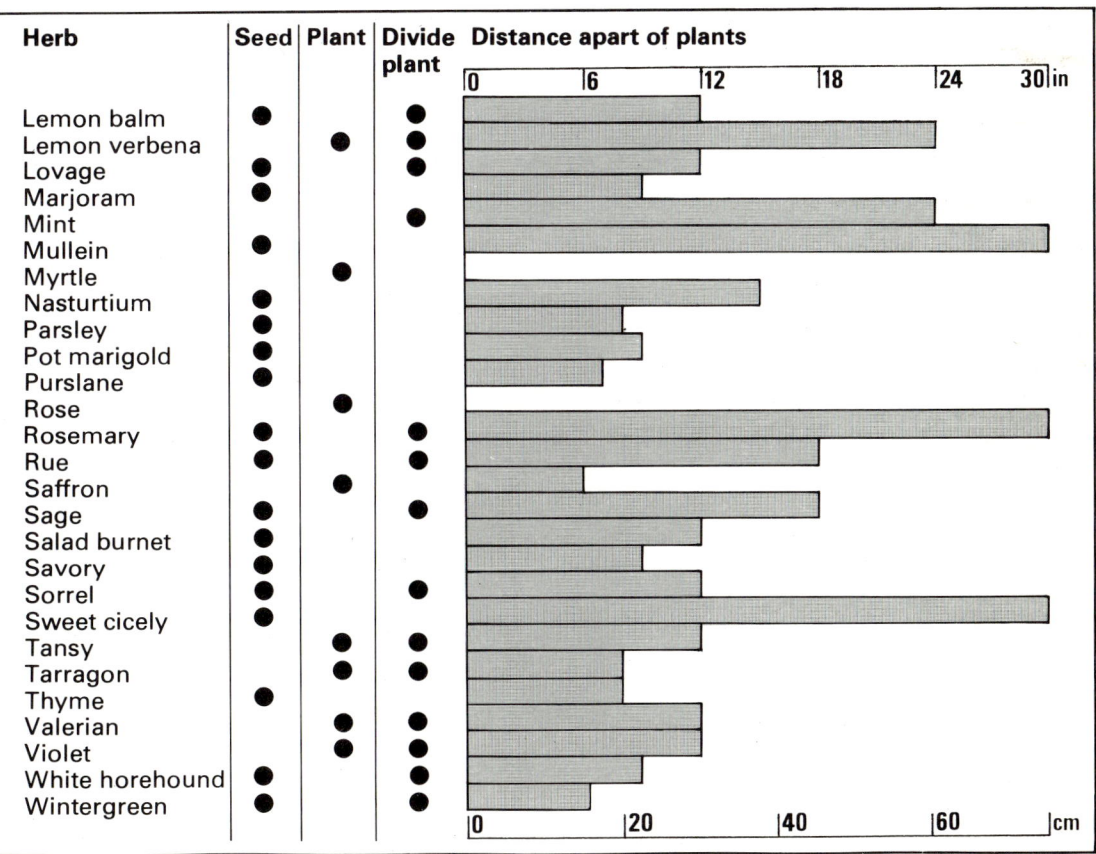

growing from seed

When you are going to sow herb seeds, it may often be advisable to start them off indoors. If you live in a flat you will have to do so anyway! But even if you have a large garden, you may decide that by choosing your time carefully you can ensure a supply of large and healthy seedlings ready to plant outdoors in the herb patch as soon as the mild weather comes, thus getting a good start to the season. If you only begin to sow seeds outside then, you will be a few weeks later to harvest.

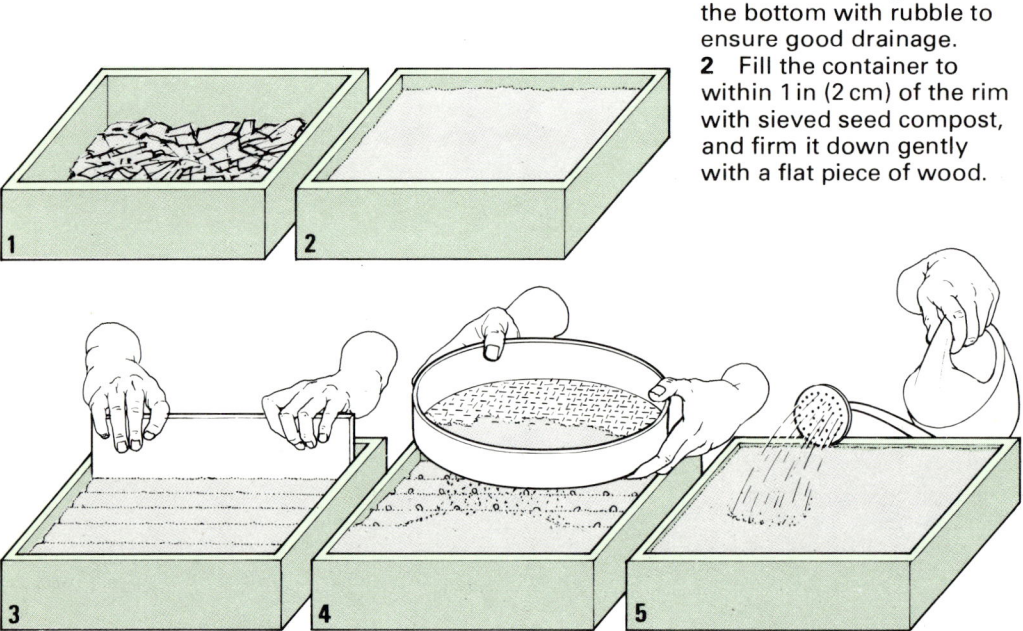

1 Make sure that boxes for sowing seeds are clean. Cover the drainage holes in the bottom with rubble to ensure good drainage.
2 Fill the container to within 1 in (2 cm) of the rim with sieved seed compost, and firm it down gently with a flat piece of wood.

3 Sprinkle the herb seeds onto the flat compost, either in lines (using a ruler as a guide) if more than one variety is being sown, or broadcast over the whole box. If the seeds are very small and hard to handle, mix them with a little silver sand, and sow the mixture. Label the seeds as you sow them, if there are several kinds.

4 Scatter a fine layer of sieved compost over the top of the seeds, but only enough just to cover them.

5 Water the whole container thoroughly, and allow to drain. Cover the top with a sheet of glass or polythene and then with a piece of thick brown paper, leaving a small gap for airing, so that the damp soil will not go mouldy. Remove the cover when shoots appear, and transplant seedlings into pots when they have one pair of leaves.

Growing herbs 19

A few plants do not like to be transplanted (eg dill), and these can be sown in peat pots. Place about 3 seeds in each pot, using the method shown opposite for sowing in boxes. When the seedlings start to look crowded together, remove the weaker ones. Later plant the peat pot with the remaining plant in the garden.

Another container for herb seeds is a cheap plastic box with a transparent lid; the bottom of the box must have small drainage holes made in it. This miniature greenhouse keeps the soil and the air around the plants humid, and excludes draughts from the tiny seedlings. Cover the box until the seeds sprout.

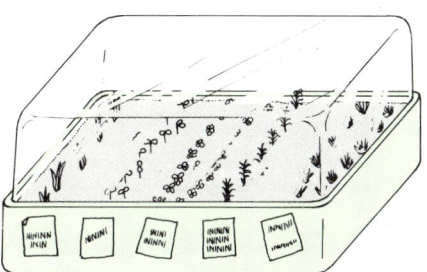

When planting seeds outside, you should prepare the bed carefully. Dig the ground and add any fertilizers it needs. Rake over the top, and make straight drills for the seeds with the back of the rake, using a string between two pegs as a guide.

1 Sow the seeds in the drills, labelling each one, and rake the soil gently over the seeds. Water thoroughly, using a watering can fitted with a rose. **2** It is a good idea to cover the seeds, and later the seedlings, with fine netting to keep birds away from them.

3 When the seedlings appear, you will have to thin them out carefully, removing the ones that look sickly and leaving the sturdiest to continue growing. (Note that the sturdiest are *not* necessarily the tallest, which are sometimes lanky.)

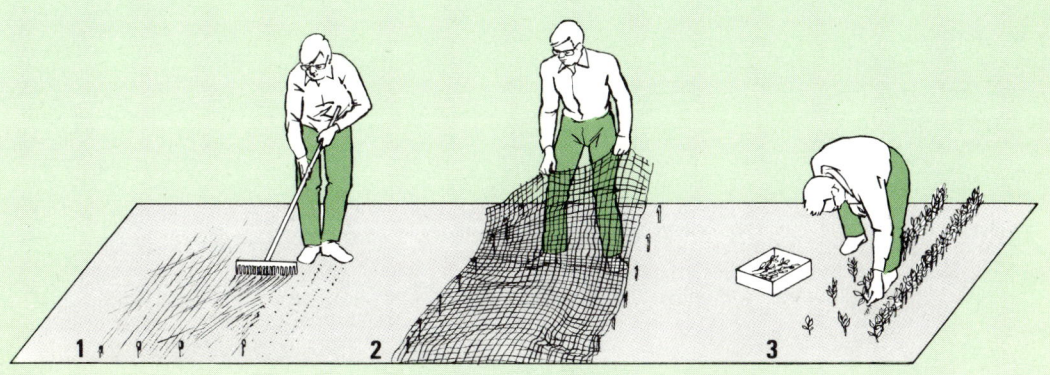

more plants

Stem cuttings
To take stem cuttings, cut healthy sprigs from the plant, between 4 and 6 in (10–15 cm) long. Remove any leaves from the bottom inch (2 cm) or so of the cutting.

Place the sprigs in a glass tumbler full of water. In a few days or a few weeks, depending which herb you are growing, tiny roots will appear on the bottom of the stem. If this takes a long time, change the water in the tumbler occasionally.

When there are a few nice little roots appearing, plant the cuttings gently in a pot full of rooting compost, firming it down and watering well.

Leaf cuttings
Instead of using a cutting several inches long, it is possible to grow a new plant from a single leaf of some varieties. Stand the leaf in a tumbler of water (supporting it if necessary, so that it is kept upright and only the leaf stem is submerged).

After an interval, the leaf will probably begin to grow little roots. Leave it, and it will also produce two tiny leaves at the base of the large one. At this point, cut off the main leaf and plant the remainder in rooting compost in a pot.

An alternative method of taking a cutting from a single leaf is this. Take a pot almost full of rooting compost, and make a hole in the compost with a pencil. Dip the end of the leaf stem in a hormone rooting powder, place the stem in the hole, and firm it in gently. Water, then cover both pot and contents with a transparent plastic bag.

Layering
A few herbs, such as rosemary, can be propagated by layering. Choose a long branch that will easily reach the soil a little away from the main plant. At a point where the branch will reach the soil, and about 9 in (23 cm) from the end of the branch, make a small cut about half way through the stem.

Strip off the leaves in the area of the cut, and dip the cut into hormone rooting powder. Bury the cut section of the branch in the soil, pegging it down so that the end of the branch is clear of the soil and almost upright.

Leave the branch undisturbed for about 10 weeks, then gently dig it up and see if any roots have formed. If it is rooting well, replace it as before, and leave for a few months before cutting the branch from the original plant and moving the new plant.

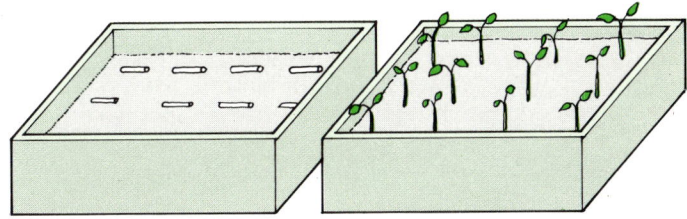

Root division
Many perennials make a lot of new growth each year. These can be simply divided into two or more small clumps, which in time will grow into large plants. Dig the whole plant up, in autumn or very early spring, and gently divide it into small bunches by hand. Plant these in pots or in the garden.

Root cuttings
Some common herbs, such as sage, lemon verbena, thyme and tarragon, can be easily propagated by root cuttings. Choose roots about ¼ in (0.5 cm) across, and cut into pieces about 2 in (5 cm) long. Plant these pieces horizontally in a pot or box of rooting compost. Cover the cuttings with ½ in (1 cm) of compost, water and cover with glass or polythene and paper. When the cuttings produce new plants, move them to individual pots or into the herb garden.

repotting

When you have had a plant in a pot for some time, it may become pot-bound: this means that the plant has grown too big for the pot it is in, and needs to be moved to a larger one. If roots begin to grow out through the drainage holes in the bottom of the pot, this is most certainly the case. But even before this, there must have been signs that all was not well: the plant needed over-frequent watering (because there was not enough soil to retain moisture), or leaves withered because of insufficient nutrients in the soil.

As soon as you discover that a plant needs to be repotted, then set to work. If you delay, the plant may die, or be so badly affected that it will never fully recover. In any case, it is a good idea to take all pot-plants out of their pots for an annual inspection, around early springtime, to make sure that they are not pot-bound. If the soil is not obviously crowded with roots, the plant can be put back into the same pot for another year.

Removing a plant from its pot
Before a plant is removed from its pot, check that the soil has been watered recently, so that it will hold around the roots when taken from the pot. If the plant has been badly neglected and there is a mass of roots outside the drainage holes, you will have to shatter the pot, or the fine roots will be damaged when you try to force them through the holes. If there is very little or no root outside, you should first put your left hand across the pot, holding the stem of the plant between your index and middle finger. Turn the pot upside down over newspaper. Tap the bottom of the pot, and the root ball may come free. If it does not come out easily, knock the pot gently against the table edge, or (only if absolutely necessary) run a knife around the inside edge of the pot to loosen the soil. Ease the soil ball from the pot; never pull it vigorously.

Growing herbs 23

Repotting
Choose a pot that is quite a lot larger than the old one. Put a crock in the bottom, and some new soil, up to the level where the bottom of the old root ball will rest. Stand the plant in the centre of its new pot, checking that the top of the soil ball will be about 1 in (2 cm) below the top of the pot. Holding the plant upright, fill in the gap around the soil ball with new compost, firming down thoroughly, and water. Alternatively, use the empty old pot and fill the new pot with fresh soil around it. Then remove the old pot and put the soil ball of the plant into the hole, firming it in, and water.

Replanting outdoors
When small seedlings are large enough, or pot plants are too large for their indoor homes, the next step is to plant them outdoors in the garden, if you have one. Before moving the plants outdoors, it is very necessary to harden them off gradually: they have been coddled indoors, shielded from draughts and kept quite warm, and the move into the big cold world outside can be fatal for them, if they are not introduced to it gradually. Choose a mild spell, and put the pots outside for an hour or two, gradually making the interval longer. When they are living outdoors all the time, and still surviving, then it is time to transplant them into the herb patch. Remove the whole soil ball from the pot as described above, then place it into a hole in the ground, being careful that the top of the soil ball is roughly level with the ground surface. Always water well.

chapter two
cultivated herbs

Mediaeval herbalists grew herbs for medical purposes.

naming herbs

It is very important to make sure that you identify herbs accurately before using them, especially if they are intended for the kitchen. For instance, fennel and finocchio are often confused because finocchio is sometimes called fennel, but the different botanical names show that they are in fact two separate species. Finocchio can be cooked as a root vegetable, but fennel cannot.

The various popular names are often only local, and it is no good asking anyone if they have seen bruisewort growing, if you are in an area where it is known as boneset: it will be much better to stick to the general name comfrey and then you will probably find some.

Once you have found your herbs, you must know which part to use: some plants have their taste or scent in the leaves, others in the seeds, flowers, stem or root. If you use the wrong part of the plant, you won't get the right result; so you should check carefully which part of the plant to use for your purpose.

HERB	BOTANICAL NAME	OTHER NAMES	🍳	⚖️	⊗	PARTS USED
Agrimony	Agrimonia eupatoria	church steeples sticklewort	🍳	⚖️		whole
Angelica	Angelica archangelica		🍳	⚖️	⊗	stem root
Anise	Pimpinella anisum		🍳	⚖️		seeds
Basil	Ocimum basilicum	sweet basil	🍳	⚖️	⊗	leaves
Bay	Laurus nobilis	Roman laurel	🍳		⊗	leaves
Bergamot	Monarda didyma	bee balm Oswego tea	🍳			
Borage	Borago officinalis	burrage	🍳	⚖️		flowers
Camomile	Anthemis nobilis	manzanilla	🍳	⚖️		flowers
Caraway	Carum carvi		🍳	⚖️		seeds
Chervil	Anthriscus cerefolium		🍳			leaves

Cultivated herbs

	HERB	This is the name by which the herb is most often known in common speech.
	BOTANICAL NAME	The botanical name may have changed over the years, but is internationally known.
	OTHER NAMES	These are often very local names for each herb, and one plant may have several.
🍳	COOKING	This symbol shows that the herb can be used in recipes to flavour foods.
🧴	SCENT	This sign shows the herbs that are used for scented toilet preparations.
⊗	POMANDERS	This shows that the herb is suitable for inclusion in pomanders and pot-pourri.
	PARTS USED	In some herbs the flower is used; in others, the leaf, stem, seed or root.

HERB	BOTANICAL NAME	OTHER NAMES	🍳	🧴	⊗	PARTS USED
Chicory	Cichorium intybus	succory	🍳			leaves root
Chives	Allium schoenoprasum		🍳			leaves
Comfrey	Symphytum officinale	bruisewort knitbone boneset		🧴		root leaves
Coriander	Coriandrum sativum		🍳	🧴		seeds
Corn salad	Valerianella olitoria	lamb's lettuce	🍳			leaves
Costmary	Tanacetum balsamita	alecost balsam herb		🧴		leaves
Cumin	Cuminum cyminum		🍳	🧴		seeds
Dill	Anethum graveolens		🍳	🧴		leaves seeds

HERB	BOTANICAL NAME	OTHER NAMES	🍳	💊	⊗	PARTS USED
Elder	Sambucus nigra	pipe tree bore tree	✓	✓	✓	flowers berries bark
Elecampane	Inula Helenium	scabwort wild sunflower	✓	✓		roots
Fennel	Foeniculum vulgare	sweet fennel	✓	✓		leaves seeds
Finocchio	Foeniculum dulce	Florence fennel	✓	✓		roots seeds leaves
Garlic	Allium sativum		✓	✓		bulb
Horseradish	Cochlearia armoracia	mountain radish	✓			root
Hyssop	Hyssopus officinalis		✓	✓	✓	leaves flowers
Juniper	Juniperus communis		✓	✓	✓	berries
Lavender	Lavandula vera Lavandula stoechas Lavandula spica				✓ ✓ ✓	flowers
Lemon balm	Melissa officinalis	sweet balm	✓	✓	✓	leaves
Lovage	Levisticum officinale		✓	✓		leaves stem seeds root
Marigold, Pot	Calendula officinalis	marygold	✓			flowers
Marjorams	Origanum vulgare Origanum marjorana Origanum onites	wild marjoram knotted marjoram pot marjoram	✓ ✓ ✓		✓	leaves leaves leaves
Mints	Mentha spicata Mentha piperita Mentha pulegium Mentha rotundifolia	spearmint peppermint pennyroyal applemint	✓ ✓ ✓	✓	✓	leaves leaves leaves leaves
Mullein	Verbascum thapsus	Jacob's staff Peter's staff		✓		flowers
Myrtle	Myrtus communis				✓	leaves flowers

Cultivated herbs

HERB	BOTANICAL NAME	OTHER NAMES	🍲	🧂	⊗	PARTS USED
Nasturtium	Tropaeolum majus		🍲			leaves seeds
Parsley	Carum petroselinum crispum	perseley	🍲			leaves
Purslane	Portulaca oleracea	pigweed	🍲			leaves
Rosemary	Rosmarinus officinalis	compass plant	🍲	🧂	⊗	leaves root
Roses	Rosa sp.		🍲	🧂	⊗	petals hips
Rue	Ruta graveolens	herb-of-grace	🍲	🧂		leaves
Saffron	Crocus sativus	crocus	🍲			stigmas of flowers
Sage	Salvia officinalis		🍲	🧂		leaves
Salad burnet	Poterium sanguisorba		🍲	🧂		leaves root
Savory	Satureia sp.		🍲		⊗	leaves
Sorrel	Rumex sp.	stickwort green sauce	🍲	🧂		leaves
Sweet cicely	Myrrhis odorata	cow chervil shepherd's needle	🍲			leaves root
Sweet violet	Viola odorata		🍲		⊗	flowers
Tansy	Tanacetum vulgare	buttons		🧂		leaves
Tarragon	Artemisia dracunculus	little dragon	🍲			leaves
Thyme	Thymus sp.		🍲	🧂	⊗	leaves flowers
Valerian	Valeriana officinalis	all-heal setwall		🧂		root
Verbena, Lemon	Lippia citriodora	herb Louisa	🍲		⊗	leaves
White horehound	Marrubium vulgare	hoarhound	🍲	🧂		leaves
Wintergreen	Gaultheria procumbens	teaberry boxberry	🍲	🧂		leaves

30 Chapter two

arrangement of chapter

PAGES

- 32 Agrimony
- 36 Angelica
- 72 Anise
- 69 Basil
- 57 Bay
- 66 Bergamot
- 40 Borage
- 37 Camomile
- 43 Caraway
- 38 Chervil
- 45 Chicory
- 34 Chives
- 82 Comfrey
- 47 Coriander
- 89 Corn salad
- 85 Costmary
- 49 Cumin
- 35 Dill
- 79 Elder
- 54 Elecampane
- 51 Fennel
- 50 Finocchio
- 33 Garlic
- 46 Horseradish
- 53 Hyssop
- 56 Juniper
- 58 Lavender
- 63 Lemon balm
- 61 Lemon verbena
- 60 Lovage
- 70 Marjorams
- 64 Mints
- 90 Mullein
- 68 Myrtle
- 87 Nasturtium
- 44 Parsley
- 42 Pot marigold
- 73 Purslane
- 74 Rose
- 75 Rosemary
- 77 Rue
- 48 Saffron
- 78 Sage
- 80 Salad burnet
- 81 Savory
- 76 Sorrel
- 67 Sweet cicely
- 84 Tansy
- 39 Tarragon
- 86 Thyme
- 88 Valerian
- 92 Violet
- 62 White horehound
- 52 Wintergreen

thyme

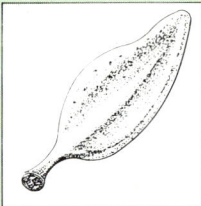

THYME. Common thyme (*Thymus vulgaris*) is one of the most popular garden herbs and better known than its relative lemon thyme (*Thymus citriodorus*). They are both small hardy evergreen shrubs, the common thyme growing to about 8 in (20 cm) high or less and the lemon variety to about 1 ft (30 cm). The common thyme has small, narrow, dark green, aromatic leaves on hard, woody stems and the plant bears very small pinkish flowers between June and August. Lemon thyme is similar in appearance, but its leaves are broader and lemon-scented and the flowers slightly darker and larger. Some varieties have golden or variegated leaves.

Both varieties may be grown from seeds or from cuttings. They like a well-drained chalky soil in a sunny position. Seeds should be sown in a cold frame, and the established seedlings transplanted into pots and planted out 1 ft (30 cm) apart in September. The plants tend to become woody in time and should be replaced every 3 or 4 years; this can be done from cuttings. The beds should be kept well weeded and well watered. Plants should be cut back in autumn and may need some protection (eg leaf mould) against frost, particularly lemon thyme. Leaves for drying should be harvested before flowering finishes.

With marjoram, parsley and a bay leaf, a sprig of common thyme makes up the traditional *bouquet garni* used for flavouring stews, soups and sauces. It is a strongly flavoured aromatic herb and should be used sparingly with other herbs: it may be included with almost any meat or fish dish and with a great many vegetables. Lemon thyme, with its additional lemon flavour, is rather more delicate. Thyme is one of the herbs used to flavour the liqueur Bénédictine. The important antiseptic thymol is extracted from its volatile oil, and essence of thyme is used in the manufacture of cosmetics.

Cultivated herbs

nasturtium

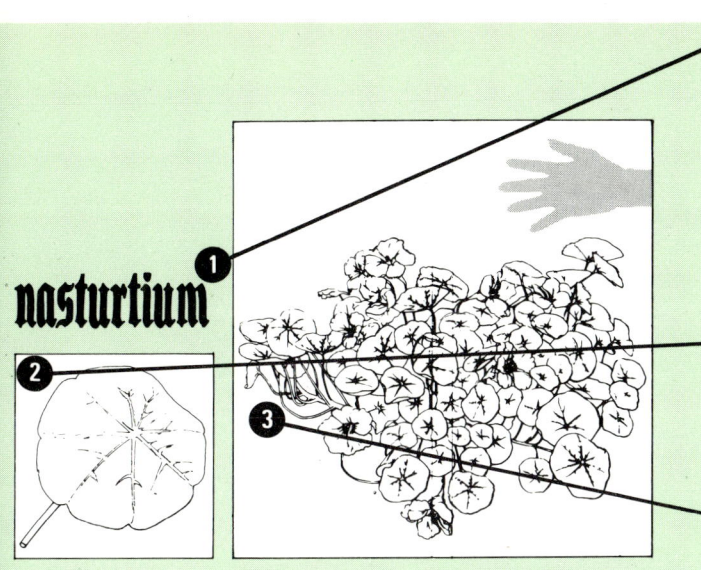

NASTURTIUM (*Tropaeolum majus*). Often grown in the flower garden, the nasturtium is a trailing or climbing annual characterized by its pale green, kidney-shaped leaves and its vivid flowers. These grow in profusion in mid-summer, are shaped like a mediaeval monk's cowl and are bright orange or yellow in colour. The flat leaves have a pungent flavour. The flowers are followed by large, pale green seeds. In the herb garden it is more convenient to plant compact varieties.

Nasturtiums like rather light soil in an open, sunny position. They are grown from seed, which is sown where the plants are to remain, but they are prolific self-seeders and once they are established it is mostly a matter of thinning out. They are naturally strong growers and no special attention is required.

The leaves have a very high Vitamin C content, but need to be used with some caution because of their hot flavour. They can be used in salads, added to cream cheese, even made into sandwiches between sliced bread and butter. The dried seeds can be ground and used as a substitute for pepper or, if pickled when young, as a substitute for capers.

1 Each of the herbs is introduced by the common name by which it is most generally known in England. Many herbs have several names – for instance, thyme is often called common thyme – but all these other names are usually included in the first column of the text below.

2 A single leaf of each separate species has been drawn, to help you to identify your plants with certainty, but this drawing is not to scale.

3 The large drawing on the right-hand side of each page shows an example of the whole plant. Plants vary in size slightly, according to the conditions under which they grow, but the woman's hand gives an idea of the scale of the foliage. It measures about 6 in (15 cm) from the wrist to the tip of the middle finger.

4 The first column of the text, includes a full description of the plant, including its leaves, stem and flowers, and the time of year when it usually blooms.

5 The second column of text describes the garden cultivation of the herb, including the conditions under which it will be most likely to thrive and the best methods of propagating the plant. It goes on to describe the harvesting: in some cases the leaves are used, in others the root or the flowers or berries.

6 The third column of text explains the various uses of the parts of the herb, some of them practicable today, others now outmoded.

agrimony

AGRIMONY (*Agrimonia eupatoria*). Sometimes called church steeples because of its spire-like spikes of yellow flowers, this widespread perennial herb grows to about 2 ft (60 cm) high. From its stiff, rough, round stem grow large, deep green leaves. In fact the size of the leaves varies all the way up the stem. The bright yellow flowers have 5 spreading petals and grow direct from the stem facing up towards the light. The fruits are covered with hooks to aid dispersal.

This herb prefers a well-drained soil and partial shade. It can be grown from seed (though this is not easy) or propagated by cuttings in spring or autumn. The plants should be about 10 in (25 cm) apart.

Agrimony has a flavour of apricots and is therefore used to flavour drinks, including cider. The whole plant is used for making agrimony tea, said to be useful as a gargle and for treating diarrhoea. The underground woody stem can also be used to make a yellow dye.

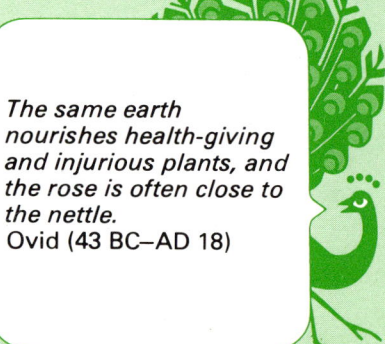

The same earth nourishes health-giving and injurious plants, and the rose is often close to the nettle.
Ovid (43 BC–AD 18)

Cultivated herbs 33

garlic

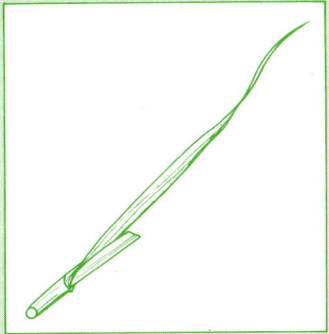

GARLIC (*Allium sativum*). This is a hardy perennial similar in some respects to the onion but with important differences. Not the least of these is the powerful, and to some disagreeable, odour of garlic. The plant itself grows to between 1 and 2 ft (30–60 cm) in height and has flat, spiky, greyish green leaves as opposed to the green, tubular leaves of the onion. It flowers in June, producing white flowers, sometimes with a touch of purple, in rather flamboyant heads. The underground bulb consists of a number of cloves held together in an onion-shaped sac of papery white skin that, when dry, flakes away. The cloves themselves break away under very slight pressure.

For sowing in spring take garlic bulbs of the previous year's growth; for autumn sowing, bulbs of that year. Each bulb contains 10 or 12 cloves. These should be carefully separated and each sown with a dibber about 2 in (5 cm) deep and 6 in (15 cm) apart in rows 1 ft (30 cm) apart. The plant likes rich, moist, slightly sandy soil exposed to the sun. It should be kept well watered and regularly weeded. Remove the flowers when in the bud stage to encourage larger bulbs. The bulbs are ready when the plant begins to wither and droop, about 5 to 6 months after planting. Dig them up, cut off the dead leaves, and hang to dry.

Apart from such traditionally attributed virtues as averting the Evil Eye, encouraging fighting cocks and discouraging moles, garlic is widely used in cooking, especially in kitchens on the European continent. Its flavour is so overwhelming and penetrating that often a clove rubbed around the dish gives enough flavour, but *afficionados* (and there are many) prefer it used far more generously. However the motto is 'Use with caution'. In herbal medicine it is regarded as helpful in throat and lung ailments. Its use in cooking is an aid to the digestion but, unshared, an enemy of romance.

chives

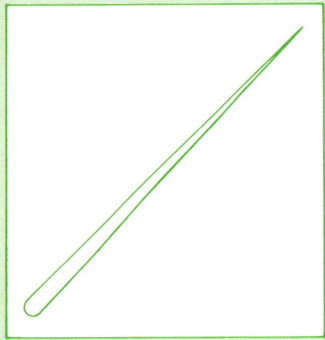

CHIVES (*Allium schoenoprasum*). Sometimes regarded as the poor man's onion, chives are hardy perennials. When growing they look a little like clumps of grass, for the small bulbs in the soil grow, flat and white, close to each other. From them grow tubular but grass-like leaves to a height of 6–9 in (15–23 cm) for the best culinary variety, although some chives can grow as high as 18 in (45 cm). A single, leafless, flowering stem bears a globular flower head, which turns more conical as the plant ripens; the flowers range from lavender to pink. The close growing of the bulbs results in attractive bunching of the flowers, so chives are useful as decorative border plants.

Growing chives does not present much difficulty. They like the sun or a partly shaded position and flourish in almost any well-drained garden soil. They can be sown outdoors in spring in shallow drills 1 ft (30 cm) apart, then thinned out and finally transplanted to their growing place about 1 ft (30 cm) apart. Once they are established, further propagation is a matter of dividing the clumps in autumn into smaller clumps of up to 6 bulbs and planting them out. The clumps go on growing, especially if they are encouraged by a top dressing of compost in the spring and are kept well watered.

Chives are quickly rewarding, for the leaves can be cut about 5 weeks after planting, and there will be a constant supply for the kitchen if the plants are cut down to about 2 in (5 cm) fairly regularly. The tiny bulbs can be used as small onions but it is the leaves that are mostly used. They have a mild onion flavour and chopped are one of the ingredients of *fines herbes*. They should be used only in the last moments of cooking, for over-cooking causes them to lose both colour and flavour.

dill

DILL (*Anethum graveolens*). This annual herb grows to about 3 ft (90 cm) in height. Usually it has a single hollow stem, which has white and green stripes and is smooth and shiny. The leaves are feathery like those of fennel but a darker green in colour. The flowers, which are yellow and formed in flat umbels, appear around July. Their petals are inward turning. Dill plants can sometimes be rather spindly. The seeds, for which the herb is mainly grown, are small, oval and flat and have three lines of oil cells.

Dill is easily grown from seeds sown in drills in March or April. The drills should be about 10 in (26 cm) apart but remember that the plant is very prolific with its seeds and don't sow too many. Seedlings should be thinned out so that the plants are not touching when fully grown. The herb prefers a dry position and grows very rapidly. Seeds should be harvested before they are completely ripe, and ripened off indoors, because they fall easily. This means, of course, that dill is very much self-seeding. If leaves are to be used they should be gathered before flowering has taken place, or from the young shoots produced afterwards.

The leaves of dill can be used fresh in soups and a variety of dishes. They can be dried, but it is not an easy process because the green colour must be retained if they are to be useful. Dill is best known for its seeds, which are used in vinegar for pickling such vegetables as gherkins, cucumbers, cabbage, onions etc. Dill water, which is made from the seeds, has been renowned through the ages for its soothing effect on children and for dispelling flatulence.

angelica

ANGELICA (*Angelica archangelica*). A tall herb indeed, garden angelica can grow over 6 ft (2 m) high. Its large, dark, bright green leaves grow from hollow stems, purplish at the base. It has small yellowish or greenish flowers formed in umbels as much as 6 in (15 cm) across. Angelica is usually regarded as a biennial as it dies after flowering but it is a perennial in the sense that it may not flower for several years. The wild variety (*Angelica sylvestris*) has white flowers and hairier stems and its flavour is less subtle than that of the garden variety.

The herb prefers damp soil in open surroundings but is tough and can stand up to most conditions. Seeds should be sown in August when they are ripe, and it is essential to use fresh seed. Even so, the seed has a poor germination rate, so plant more than you need. Seeds can be sown either where they are to remain or in seed beds for transplanting the following summer. Remember that the plants are not only tall but wide, and eventually they should be at least 3 ft (1 m) apart. The herb is harvested in June before it has flowered and both leaves and young stems are gathered.

The best-known form of angelica is the dark green stem, cooked in sugar and candied and used by confectioners. The stems should be cut in 5 in (12 cm) lengths, covered with boiling syrup and left for a day, then boiled up again until the stems turn bright green as they are cooked. Thicker stems may be cooked with rhubarb or used to flavour jams, and the seeds are used to flavour wines and liqueurs. In herbal medicine it has long been regarded as useful against stomach disorders and as an expectorant and in ancient days was thought to be an antidote to the plague.

camomile

CAMOMILE (*Anthemis nobilis*). This fragrant herb, often spelled chamomile, smells slightly of apples; its name derives from the Greek for ground (*chamai*) and for apple (*melon*).
A non-flowering variety is often used for lawns, and has been for centuries. An old rhyme says 'Like a camomile bed, The more it is trodden the more it will spread', and one of the charms of the camomile lawn is that when it is walked on, the plant exudes its characteristic fragrance. Camomile has a slightly feathery appearance and is a rich green; flowering varieties produce large white flowers in summer. A hardy perennial, it spreads from 12 to 15 in (30–37 cm) and reaches less than 9 in (23 cm) in height.

Camomile can be grown outdoors from seed in April, in well-drained, preferably rather dry, sandy soil. When they are large enough to handle, thin the seedlings out or transplant them about 18 in (45 cm) apart for herbal use only, or 6 in (15 cm) apart for a lawn where they are to grow. They should be pressed in firmly. Keep well weeded by hand. Once established they will produce runners from which more plants can be propagated. The old plants with their runners should be divided in March.

Double camomile should be used for making tea; the single variety is coarse. To make a very refreshing tisane, 1 oz (28 gm) of the camomile flowers should be infused in 1 pt (0.5 l) of boiling water. The tisane has a soothing effect on the nerves. The flowers are also used in medicine and to make a lotion for external use in the relief of skin irritation. In Spain they are used to flavour wine, whence the name for a light sherry, *Manzanilla* (little apple).

Camomile
Though the Camomill, the more it is trodden and pressed down the more it spreadeth.
John Lyly (1533–1606) — *Euphues*

chervil

CHERVIL (*Anthriscus cerefolium*). This very decorative hardy annual grows to between 1 and 1½ ft (30–45 cm) high and has dainty, bright green leaves not unlike those of parsley. Indeed its aroma and flavour are not dissimilar. The plant has a white tapering root smelling slightly of aniseed, stands erect with ridged, hollow stems, and has a spread of about 1 ft (30 cm). It flowers from June to late summer with very small white blossoms in flat lacy heads, and later in the year the stalks and leaves turn first mauve and then red.

Chervil should be sown at intervals from February to August to ensure succession. You can sow it in almost any soil except a very heavy one but it does like some shade as it dislikes hot, dry conditions. Sow in drills 1 ft (30 cm) apart where it is to grow. Weed and water well, thinning out the seedlings when 2–3 in (5–8 cm) high, to 9 in (23 cm) apart. Once established they will self-seed. Pick the flowers as soon as they appear or the stalks will shoot rapidly. The leaves can generally be cut 6 to 8 weeks after sowing. When you gather them cut the plant down to the ground and more growth will occur.

Chervil is one of the most important ingredients of *fines herbes*. The fresh young leaves are used generously in sauces and salads and, chopped, in many dishes, particularly those made with fish or eggs. They are added at the later stage of cooking to preserve their colour. They can also be used dried, but with carefully planned sowing and the use of cloches or frames a supply of fresh leaves can be assured for most of the year. If you have a greenhouse you can sow from October to February at a temperature of 45–50°F (7–10°C).

tarragon

TARRAGON (*Artemisia dracunculus*). There are two varieties of this perennial herb, the French and the Russian. The more popular and more frequently grown, because of its finer flavour, is the French variety. This grows to a height of about 3 ft (90 cm) and has narrow, dark green, shiny leaves, slightly paler on the underside. The leaves are widely spaced on the slender stems, giving the herb a slightly feathery appearance. Yellow-grey flowers appear in clusters in mid-summer but in Britain they hardly ever open fully. The Russian variety has paler, less glossy leaves and can grow as much as 2 ft (60 cm) taller than the French one; it has a poor flavour, and is extremely invasive.

You don't need much tarragon in your garden, because a little goes a long way: probably not more than a couple of plants are required. The herb likes a very well-drained, light soil in a warm, sunny position. Remember that it has a widely spreading root system: plants should therefore be at least 2 ft (60 cm) apart. Propagation is from division of roots or by cuttings, and planting can be either in spring, when the danger of frost is past, or in September. Plants should be cut down with the approach of winter and some protection of the roots by mulching may be necessary.

Tarragon leaves can be used either fresh or dried. Their flavour is at its best just before flowering, in late June or early July. The herb is widely used in cooking, especially in sauces (Hollandaise and Tartare), with roast chicken and shellfish and in many other dishes. It is an ingredient of French mustard and, of course, of tarragon vinegar, which is made by putting the leaves in bottles of white wine vinegar.

borage

BORAGE (*Borago officinalis*). Beloved by bees for its blue flowers, borage, a hardy annual, is easily recognized. It grows from 1½ to 3 ft (45–90 cm) high and has a hollow stem with large wrinkled lower leaves about 3 in (7 cm) long and half that in width, oval and pointed. But the chief characteristic of the plant is its hairiness. Stems, leaves and flower buds are all covered with short silvery hairs. Borage flowers in May or June depending whether it was planted in the previous autumn or in the spring. The small fine-petalled flowers are a bright blue with black anthers. Bees are greatly attracted to them and bee-keepers plant borage for this reason.

Once it is established borage requires little cultivation as such, for it grows strongly and prolifically, seeding itself. The main problem once it is established is keeping it down. It can be grown from seed sown out of doors in April or May and flourishes in most soils, although it prefers light soil. Seed drills should be 18 in (45 cm) apart and the seedlings should be thinned out to 15 in (37 cm) apart. Further sowing should not be needed: you will find dozens of small plants showing, the following spring. For harvesting see next column. If borage is planted beside strawberries, both plants seem to gain in growth and in flavour.

Borage is used as a decoration and flavouring for summer drinks, such as Pimm's No 1 Cup. It has a fresh fragrance somewhat reminiscent of cucumber, and a sprig, with its attractive blue flowers, greatly enhances both the taste and the appearance of a fruit cup. The young leaves can be used in salads or cooked like spinach, and the flowers, picked just before they open, can be crystallized and used as a cake decoration. In herbal medicine borage has the reputation of stimulating both mind and spirit, and in Europe a tisane is often made with its flowers.

Cultivated herbs

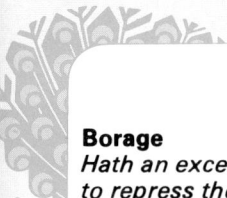

Borage
Hath an excellent spirit to repress the fuliginous vapour of dusky melancholie.
Bacon (1561–1626)

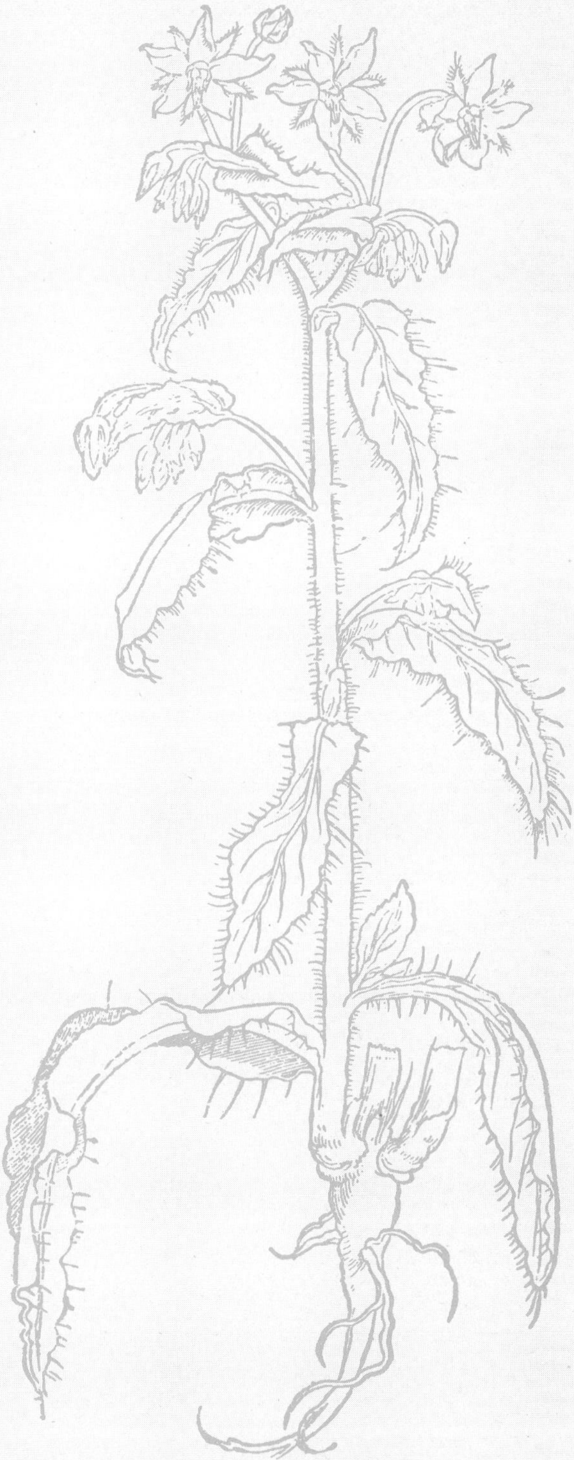

pot marigold

POT MARIGOLD (*Calendula officinalis*). This comparatively small annual is a useful inhabitant of the herb garden because it flowers (as its Latin name indicates) for a long period – in Britain, some 7 or 8 months. It grows to nearly 2 ft (60 cm) high and has shiny, stalkless, pale green, rather spoon-shaped leaves. The plant has single vivid orange or saffron-coloured flowers, which can appear as early as April and continue until late autumn.

The marigold is not choosy about the soil in which it grows, so long as it is in an open, sunny position. Seeds can be sown in spring where they are to grow and should be thinned out to about 18 in (45 cm) apart to help make a bushy growth. The flowers should be picked regularly as this will help to prolong the flowering period.

It is the flower petals that are used, not only for their subtle flavour but also for colouring different dishes. They have to be dried carefully, by spreading them on paper in a warm atmosphere out of the sunlight, if they are to retain their colour. Because of this strong yellow colour they are sometimes used as a substitute for saffron. They can also be used to flavour salads and meat and fish dishes.

Marigold
*Open afresh your round of starry folds
Ye ardent Marigolds.
Keats (1795–1821) — I Stood Tip-toe*

caraway

CARAWAY (*Carum carvi*). This hardy biennial herb grows to a height of 3 ft (90 cm) and has yellow-green, fern-like leaves not unlike those of carrots, on smooth, grooved stems. The flowers, tiny and white, appear in umbels about 1½–2 in (3–5 cm) across in June. The plant dies down during winter and seeds in its second year. The small seeds, for which the plant is grown, are slightly sickle-shaped and translucent with pale ridges and they have a distinctive aroma when crushed. The plant's thick roots are carrot-shaped.

Caraway can be grown from seed sown where the plants are to grow, which should be in well-drained light soil in a sunny position. They should be sown in shallow drills and the seedlings, when large enough to handle, thinned out first to 6 in (15 cm), then to 1 ft (30 cm) apart. Seeds can be sown in March but sowing is best with newly ripe seeds in autumn. Little cultivation is needed beyond occasional hoeing between rows. Harvesting takes place when the seeds are fully ripe and tend to fall from the plant. The heads should be carefully taken off and hung over paper or in bags to catch the seeds as they fall.

The dried seeds of the herb, with their characteristic flavour, are used to add relish to salads, cheeses, bread and cakes; a favourite cake in Britain was flavoured with caraway seeds and known simply as 'seed cake'. One Cambridge college preserves the tradition of serving baked apple with caraway seeds on the side (in Shakespeare's *Henry IV*, Falstaff is invited to eat 'a pippin and a dish of caraways'). Caraway gives its flavour to the liqueur Kummel and is used in other cordials. In herbal medicine its oil is used as a remedy for indigestion.

parsley

PARSLEY (*Carum petroselinum crispum*). The most popular variety of this herb is the curled garden parsley, identifiable by its densely curled, crisp, bright green leaves. It is a hardy biennial, but its leaves are best in the first year and it is usually grown as an annual. The plant grows to 1–2 ft (30–60 cm) and the leaves are borne on hollow stems. In the second year the plant bears clusters of small white or yellow-green flowers, which should be removed to keep leaf growth going. The less popular fern-leaf variety (sometimes known as French parsley) has deeply divided leaves, but they are flat. Hamburg parsley (*Carum petroselinum fusiformis*) has leaves that are of poorer flavour.

Garden parsley seeds may take from 5 to 8 weeks to germinate and it is a good tip to mix a few lettuce or radish seeds in when sowing. These germinate much more quickly, and mark the rows. Sow in March in shallow drills 1 ft (30 cm) apart. Because of the slow germination it is important that the soil should be kept moist. As soon as the seedlings are large enough to handle, thin them out to 3 in (8 cm) and later to 9 in (23 cm) apart. Keep the plants watered in dry weather. Remove flower stems when they appear. Cover with cloches in the winter. To ensure a continual supply make 2 or 3 sowings each year. Hamburg parsley is sown and thinned in the same way.

Garden parsley leaves have a mild but distinctive flavour and are widely used in the kitchen. Moreover its bright colour and crisp leaves make it a splendid garnish. Parsley is an essential ingredient of the traditional *bouquet garni* and *fines herbes*. Chopped, the leaves are used to make parsley sauce, parsley butter etc, and to flavour and garnish new potatoes; they can also be used in salads, buttered eggs and many other dishes. Parsley tea can be made with 1 teaspoon of dried leaves to 1 cup of boiling water. The roots of Hamburg parsley can be boiled like parsnips, grated raw in salads or added to stews. In herbal medicine parsley is used for kidney complications. It is rich in Vitamins A and C.

chicory

CHICORY (*Cichorium intybus*). The chicory you see growing in the garden bears no resemblance to the pale white salad you buy from the greengrocer. The plant, a perennial, grows to 3 ft (90 cm) high or more. The stem bears large, hairy leaves and these become much smaller and more sparse up the stem. The plant has spreading branches but these do not carry many leaves. It blooms from July to September, the flowers being a delicate blue in colour, nearly 2 in (4 cm) across. In sunshine they open only in the morning. The plant is also used as fodder for animals.

Seeds can be sown in May or June in 1 in (2 cm) drills 1 ft (30 cm) apart, and the seedlings thinned out to 8 in (20 cm) apart. They should be kept well watered. To obtain the familiar salad the roots should be lifted in mid-autumn and the tops removed. The roots are then replanted, packed closely together in deep boxes, leaving a space of 6–8 in (15–20 cm) between the top of the soil and the top of the box. The box is then covered and kept in the dark for several weeks, during which time new, tightly packed leaves grow, torch-shaped, from the root and are blanched by the absence of light.

The foliage thus produced makes an excellent, crisp winter salad and can also be boiled as a vegetable. The roots, roasted and ground, are used to flavour coffee.

Chicory
A fine, cleansing, jovial plant.
Parkinson (1567–1650)

horseradish

HORSERADISH (*Cochlearia armoracia*). This hardy perennial grows vigorously and if not kept in check gets out of hand. Its leaves are not unlike those of the dock but they are larger, darker and glossier. They can reach a height of 2 ft (60 cm) and the plant can reach the same width. It bears small white flowers with four petals in early summer. Horseradish is grown not for its leaves but for its long white tap root.

The plant can be propagated in rich, moist soil from seed sown in early spring or by planting sections of root. Seedlings should be thinned out to 1 ft (30 cm) apart, and root sections planted the same distance apart. If planting root pieces, dig a short trench 2 ft (60 cm) deep, put in some manure or compost, return the topsoil to about 4 in (10 cm) from the top and lay the root pieces 1 ft (30 cm) apart on this. Cover with the remaining soil. The roots take 2 years to mature. Horseradish is so vigorous that it is best grown in a container or treated as an annual. If you are trying to get rid of your horseradish, dig out every piece of root.

Only the long root of the horseradish is used in the kitchen. It has an extremely hot and pungent flavour and is always grated or cut in very thin strips and usually mixed with a white cream sauce. It is most familiar as an accompaniment to roast beef, but can be used with smoked fish and other dishes. It has to be used very sparingly because of its burning pungency and is often mixed with other herbs to reduce this.

coriander

CORIANDER (*Coriandrum sativum*). This annual, which grows up to 3 ft (90 cm) high, is chiefly remarkable for its disagreeable smell. Its bright green leaves vary according to their position on the erect stems: those at the top are so divided as to look feathery, but those below are stalked and roundish, though with indentations. It flowers in June or July in short-stalked umbels, the flowers being white, pale lilac or pink. They are followed by globular, sandy-coloured, ribbed seeds.

Seeds can be sown in ½ in (1 cm) drills outdoors in April. The drills should be 9 in (22 cm) apart. Or the seeds may be sown under glass to be planted out in May about 1½ ft (45 cm) apart. The plant likes a sunny position with well-drained soil. The seeds begin to ripen about August and as they do so their unpleasant smell begins to disappear, to be replaced by a more agreeable aroma. When this has happened the plant should be cut down and the seeds shaken off for use.

Like the seed of caraway, coriander seeds are used to flavour breads and cakes. They are also used in curries and are an important ingredient for making pickling vinegar. Curiously, despite the disagreeable odour associated with them when they are unripe, the oil extracted from them is often used to disguise the otherwise disagreeable flavour of some medicines.

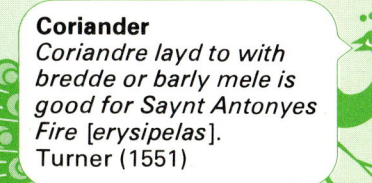

Coriander
Coriandre layd to with bredde or barly mele is good for Saynt Antonyes Fire [erysipelas].
Turner (1551)

saffron

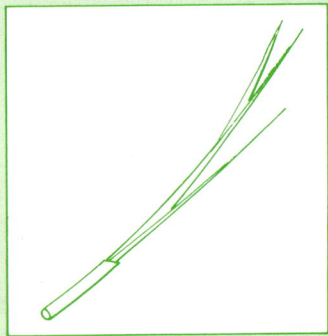

SAFFRON (*Crocus sativus*). There are many varieties of crocus to be seen in parks and gardens in the spring but it is the *Crocus sativus* that gives us the dye saffron. It is a bulbous plant, low-growing and with leaves rather like grass. In the middle of the leaves grow open purple flowers like lilies with pronounced yellow pistils. The flowers bloom in October. The saffron crocus is a favourite meal for mice, so avoid planting it near a mouse-infested rockery.

Strangely enough, although the saffron crocus was once widely cultivated in Britain (whence the place name Saffron Walden), today it seems to be too difficult to grow there. It requires a good hot summer to bring it to maturity. It grows from corms, which are planted 2–3 in (5–7 cm) deep about 6 in (15 cm) apart. The yellow stigmas are picked from the flowers in autumn and dried into a cake under pressure. The corms, which will have multiplied, should be raised after the third year and transplanted.

Saffron is cultivated commercially for its yellow colouring. This is used as a dye for clothing and in cooking, where it also imparts a slight flavour. Saffron cakes and rice coloured with it are perhaps the best-known ways in which it is used.

Crocus
Lowly, with a broken neck,
The crocus lays her cheek to mire.
George Meredith
(1828–1909)

Cultivated herbs

cumin

CUMIN (*Cuminum cyminum*). This small annual herb looks very delicate against the tougher inhabitants of the herb garden. Its slender, rather weak-looking stems grow to a height of less than 1 ft (30 cm) and carry long, dark green leaves not unlike those of fennel. The upper leaves have very little stalk. Its flowers appear in June or July and are white or rose-coloured, growing in umbels at the head of the stems. They are followed by oblong seeds, rather like the seeds of caraway but not so dark.

Seeds can be sown under glass in small pots, and the seedlings hardened off and planted out where they are to grow, about 9 in (23 cm) apart. Cumin likes a good breathing space with plenty of sun and should not be crowded by other plants. It should be kept weed free. It is mentioned in the Bible and originated in Egypt, hence its requirement of warm sunlight. Seeds are unlikely to mature in a cold summer in Britain. When ripe the seeds are shaken from the plant and dried, as with caraway seeds.

At one time the aromatic seeds of cumin, ground or whole, were used for culinary flavouring. Today it is used mostly in veterinary medicine.

Cumin
Woe unto you – for ye pay tithe of mint and anise and cumin.
Matthew XXIII 23

finocchio

FINOCCHIO or FLORENCE FENNEL (*Foeniculum dulce*). Although it too is a fennel, finocchio is a very different plant from the common fennel (*Foeniculum vulgare*). It is an annual and does not grow so high as its namesake, reaching only about 2½ ft (75 cm). Its leaves can be used in the same way as those of common fennel but it is grown mainly for the bulbous base that develops in its stem. The base swells naturally, the stalk becoming thicker and wider and the leaves overlapping. The base is crisp and has the flavour of aniseed.

This herb is sown in shallow drills in early autumn in a prepared seed bed and, when big enough to handle, pricked out to 12 in (30 cm) apart. Or it can be sown in spring where it is to grow. It is not greatly demanding as to soil but likes fairly moist conditions and must be kept well watered and free of weeds. As the base swells the plants should be fed and earth should be drawn up around them to blanch the base. The swollen base should be cut cleanly away from the roots when it is lifted. In the autumn plants can be transplanted into pots and kept indoors.

The leaves and seeds of finocchio are used in cooking in very much the same way as those of the common fennel: that is, in soups and salads, meat and fish dishes, etc. But the swollen stems are a bonus. They can be sliced thinly and served with green salad, or cut in half, boiled, covered with white sauce and grated cheese and browned under the grill. The herb contains similar volatile oils to those of common fennel, and these are put to pharmaceutical use.

fennel

FENNEL (*Foeniculum vulgare*). This — common fennel — is a handsome perennial that can be grown to good effect in the flower border. It grows to a height of some 4 or 5 ft (1.2–1.5 m) and has strong, shiny, bright green stems bearing a profusion of fine lace-like leaves. Its appearance is very similar (see below) to that of dill. When young the leaves are a light green, but become darker and more blue later. In July and August its golden-yellow flowers are borne on flat umbels up to 6 in (15 cm) across. There is also a handsome bronze variety, which is equally good for cooking. The root is a yellowish white and looks something like that of the horseradish.

Fennel is grown from seed sown in spring and seedlings should be thinned out to about 15 in (37 cm) apart. Do not sow or grow near dill, which is very similar, because cross-pollination between the two can produce useless plants. The falling seeds of fennel provide a constant supply of new plants and little cultivation is required. If the plants are cut back regularly through the summer fresh young leaves will grow abundantly. Fennel prefers a warm position but is not choosy about the soil in which it grows. Stake or shelter the tall varieties from the wind.

The leaves of fennel are used, chopped or whole, cooked or raw, in soups and salads and in the flavouring of meat and fish. Young leaves can be used as a salad and the pale, lime-green seeds can be used to flavour cheese and bread: they have a faint aroma of anise. In medicine, fennel is an ingredient of gripe water and the seeds are used to make a pleasant soothing tisane. But to the ancients and in herbal medicine today its main virtue is thought to be its beneficial effects on the eyes, when used as a lotion.

wintergreen

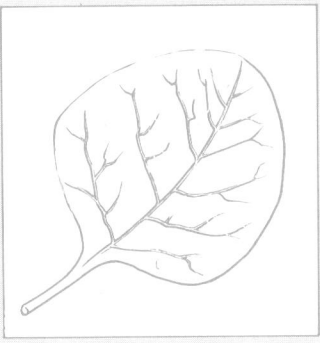

WINTERGREEN (*Gaultheria procumbens*). This is a very low-growing evergreen flowering shrub, which does not reach a height of more than 6 in (15 cm). It has curled, bright green, shiny leaves, rather leathery-looking and paler on the lower side. They grow from stiff stems and are pointed. The flower stems grow from the base of the leaves and produce tiny white or pink, waxy-looking, drooping flowers in June and July. These are followed by bright red berries. It is a spreading plant and therefore provides good ground cover, looking well in rock gardens and borders. Wintergreen much prefers an acid, peaty soil in which to grow.

The herb can be grown from seed or from heeled cuttings taken in mid-summer, the latter method being easier. Cuttings, about 3 in (8 cm) long, should be planted in a mixture of peat and sand, kept in a cold frame over the winter, potted in a mixture of peat, loam and sand and planted outdoors until autumn. They can then be planted out in their growing positions. When growing from seed (taken from the berries), sow in seed boxes of sand and peat in autumn and keep in a cold frame, pricking out the seedlings when large enough to handle in a nursery bed. Keep them there for a year or two before planting out in final growing positions.

The leaves of wintergreen contain a volatile oil that is well-known to athletes in the form of embrocation, for it helps to alleviate muscular stiffness, swellings and rheumatic pains. The herb has no culinary uses, but in some countries both leaves and berries are used to make an infusion drunk as a substitute for tea. In Quebec, wintergreen is known as *thé de Canada*.

hyssop

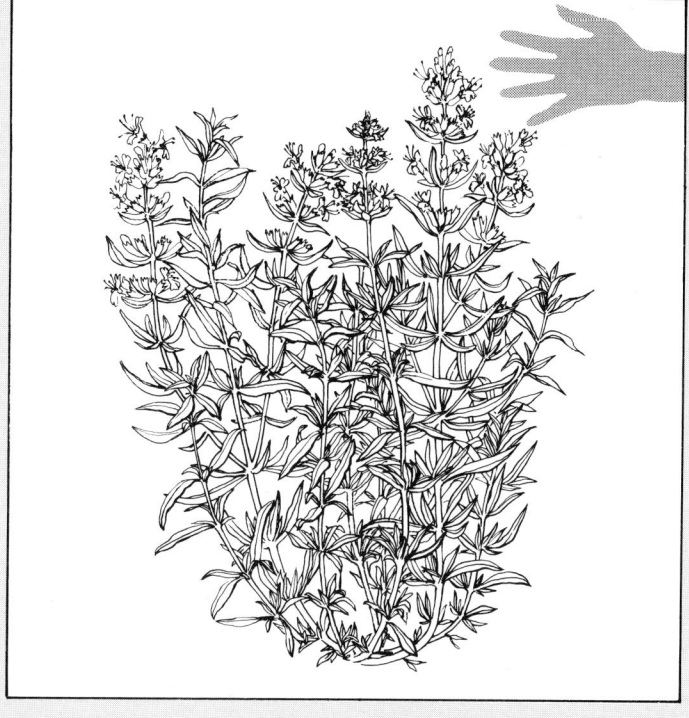

HYSSOP (*Hyssopus officinalis*). This herb, which is mentioned in the Bible, grows as a small shrub about 2 ft (60 cm) high in cold areas and between 2 and 4 ft (60–120 cm) in others. It is an evergreen perennial with a squarish stem and narrow green leaves, and it flowers from June to August. The flowers are borne on one side of curved spikes and are normally a very bright blue although there are pink and white varieties. The plant has a refreshing fragrance and is much liked by bees and butterflies: it can be grown to distract the cabbage butterfly from its natural food. Hyssop is decorative in a flower border and can be kept trim as a border by clipping.

Hyssop can be raised from either seed or cuttings. Sowing, in shallow drills about 1 ft (30 cm) apart, should be in April and when the seedlings are big enough to handle they should be thinned or planted out about 1 ft (30 cm) apart. The plants prefer a light soil in plenty of sunshine. Cuttings should be taken in the spring, and kept well watered until they have established themselves, but they do not require much cultivation after that. Leaves for use in cooking should be cut before the plant flowers.

The leaves of hyssop have a slightly bitter taste of mint, and when young can be used finely chopped in meat dishes, stews and soups. The dried flowers are used in an infusion to make hyssop tea, said to be good for weak chests, and the green tops, also in an infusion, are said to be good for weak stomachs. Oil from hyssop is in great demand for the manufacture of scent, soaps etc, and is also used to flavour liqueurs, one of the best-known of these being Chartreuse.

Hyssop
Purge me with Hyssop and I shall be clean.
Psalms LI, 7

elecampane

ELECAMPANE (*Inula Helenium*). This hardy perennial, one of the larger of the herbs, is impressive to look at, especially when it is in bloom. It grows to a height of 5 ft (1.5 m), and has strong, deeply grooved, erect stems with huge stalked leaves over 1 ft (30 cm) long at the base and smaller leaves that clasp the stem higher up. The bright yellow flowers, which develop at the end of the stems from June to August, can be over 3 in (8 cm) in diameter and resemble sunflowers.

Although cultivation is not difficult, the herb is little cultivated in Britain although it is common in Europe. It can be grown either from seeds sown in the open in spring or from root sections taken in the autumn. Seedlings should be planted out about 10 in (26 cm) apart in rows 1 ft (30 cm) apart, as should the root sections if propagated in this fashion. It likes a good, loamy, moist soil in a shady position and should be kept well weeded.

Elecampane is grown for its large, fleshy roots. These used to be made into a sort of candy said to be good for asthma. The root is also used in the manufacture of the drink absinthe. But two of its country names — scabwort and horseheal — indicate pretty clearly its use in the veterinary world as a medicine for sheep and horses.

> **Elecampane**
> *Julia Augusta let no day pass without eating some of the roots of Enula, considered to help digestion and cause mirth.*
> Pliny (AD 23–79)

juniper

JUNIPER (*Juniperus communis*). This evergreen shrub can be found growing wild but gardeners who have room cultivate it successfully. Its height ranges from 4 to 12 ft (1.2–3.6 m). Its grey-green leaves, growing from reddish stems, are needle-shaped, not unlike those of the pine, and have a white line on the underside. Its small yellow flowers appear at the base of the leaves in April and May. Berries are produced only by female plants. They are green at first, turning blackish when ripe.

The shrub can be grown from seed, sown in autumn in seed compost and overwintered in potting compost. When big enough to handle, the seedlings should be planted out in a nursery bed, where they should be allowed to grow for a year or two before they are transplanted to their permanent stations. They will grow in most garden soils but those that grow wild seem to flourish best on chalky sites. The berries, which should be gathered only when black, are harvested in autumn.

The dried berries can be used in the kitchen with game and rich meat dishes, in sauces and in pickling vinegar. From them is extracted a volatile oil that is used to flavour gin. In herbal medicine they are made into a tea reputed to be valuable in the treatment of kidney and liver conditions. The young shoots of the juniper, after boiling, can be used as a bath essence.

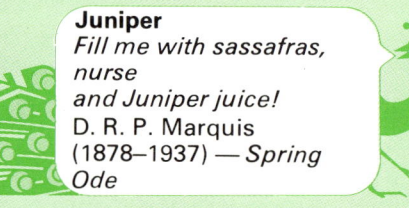

Juniper
*Fill me with sassafras, nurse
and Juniper juice!*
D. R. P. Marquis (1878–1937) — *Spring Ode*

bay

BAY (*Laurus nobilis*). This is a small laurel tree, which can grow to a height of over 20 ft (6 m), but when cultivated is usually kept down to about 6 ft (2 m) or is frequently grown, neatly trimmed in tubs, as a bush. It comes originally from the Mediterranean but flourishes in Britain and other countries with cooler climates. It is an evergreen bearing shiny, pointed, dark green leaves sometimes as long as 4 in (10 cm), which are a paler, greyish green underneath. The bark of the tree can be greenish or reddish. Small inconspicuous clusters of yellow-green flowers appear in April or May and these are sometimes followed by black or dark purple ovoid berries.

The bay laurel is best grown in a sheltered spot away from north and east winds and where the ground is well-drained. The trees are not easy to grow and take some years to mature. They are usually propagated from cuttings in late summer or by layering a low branch. The cuttings are potted in an equal mixture of peat and sand in a cold frame, potted on when rooted, and planted out in October. They need to grow for another two years before they become finally established where they are to grow.

In cooking the bay leaf is always used dried. Leaves can be picked all the year round and as they tend to curl should be pressed for a few days after drying. With parsley and thyme a bay leaf is a traditional ingredient of a *bouquet garni* used for flavouring stews, sauces, soups etc. The bay leaf is also used by itself for flavouring, but the flavour from its volatile oil is extremely strong and it should be used sparingly. The oil of the herb is used in the manufacture of oriental perfumes. In medicine it is used to alleviate strains and bruises.

lavender

LAVENDER. This herb, cultivated entirely for its perfume, is familiar in both flower and herb garden. There are several varieties, the most common of which is known as English lavender (*Lavandula vera*). Others are French lavender (*Lavandula stoechas*) and spike lavender (*Lavandula spica*). English lavender grows up to 3 ft (90 cm) high. It is an evergreen shrub with a short jagged stem, with grey bark that peels off, from which many branches grow. These branches bear narrow silver-grey leaves and — from July to September — spikes of small flowers. The fragrant oil for which lavender is famous is produced from only the flowers and their stalks.

Propagation is usually from cuttings. These may be taken in August as ripe, non-flowering shoots about 4 in (10 cm) long and kept in a cold frame during the winter. Or more mature cuttings, 7–8 in (18–20 cm) long, may be taken a month later and planted out where they are to grow. The plants will grow in most well-drained soils in a sunny position and should be planted about 15 in (37 cm) apart. For drying, gather the flowers when the colour shows without waiting for them to open. The flower stems should be removed as they fade, and the plant trimmed in late summer and pruned to encourage growth in March.

Lavender is the perfumer's plant. Its fragrant oil is used in perfumes, cosmetics and soap and the plant is often grown to attract bees. The Latin name *Lavandula* is related to cleanliness, for lavender was used in their baths by the ancient Romans. Dried flowers are included in pot-pourri and in small sachets for fragrant storage of linen. Oil of lavender is an insect deterrent.

lovage

LOVAGE (*Levisticum officinale*). This is one of the taller perennial herbs, sometimes reaching a height of 5 ft (1.5 m). It is something like angelica, with a similar hollow stem, but it has large, dark green leaves not unlike those of celery, and something of a celery flavour. In June or July it bears large umbels, nearly 5 in (13 cm) across, of velvety yellow flowers, which give way to very aromatic elliptical curved seeds that are brown when ripe. The plant has a short carrot-like root with long rootlets. Scottish lovage (*Levisticum Scoticum*) grows wild, is a good deal shorter, and has white or pink flowers.

Lovage can be grown either by dividing existing plants or from seeds. Although one plant may be enough for the garden it is as well to sow fairly generously in the autumn after the seeds are ripe, because although lovage is strong when once established, not all the seed germinate. Seedlings should be spaced out early in spring where they are to grow, about 2 ft (60 cm) apart and thinned to 4 ft (1.2 m) apart when fully grown, ie about 4 years after sowing. Lovage likes a rich, moist soil, and is unhappy in heavy clay. It should be kept well watered and prevented from seeding if the flowers are to be used in the kitchen.

Correctly dried at a very low temperature the leaves will keep their green colour and can be shredded for storage in airtight containers out of the light. Either fresh or dried they can be used for flavouring a wide range of dishes from salads to poultry and meat. The stems can be candied like those of angelica but they are not so fine: the seeds are sometimes sprinkled over loaves of bread or biscuits. Lovage, a cordial flavoured with this herb, was once very popular in British inns. A herbal tea is also made from the leaves.

lemon verbena

VERBENA, LEMON (*Lippia citriodora*). This is another of the larger inhabitants of the herb garden, a deciduous shrub that can grow as high as 15 ft (4.6 m). Its pale green leaves (which feel slightly sticky) are highly fragrant, exuding an aroma of lemon even when only lightly touched. They are large and pointed, 3 to 4 in (7–10 cm) long, and grow in threes from the stem. The shrub flowers in August with spikes of small mauve blossoms growing at the end of the stems. The leaves are most highly scented just before the plant flowers.

Lemon verbena likes fertile, well-drained soil in a sunny sheltered position; it is not suitable for growing in the north of Britain. It should be planted late in May, or cuttings may be taken in July into equal parts of peat and sand and kept in mild heat until the following May when they are planted out in their growing positions. The main growths should be pruned back in April as well as the lateral growths, which should be cut back to 2 or 3 buds. The lemon-scented leaves should be gathered when the shrub flowers.

Although the dried or fresh leaves can be used to make a soothing tisane, and to flavour some dishes, they are used mainly in perfumery, in sachets for storing linen, and in pot-pourri.

> Lift your boughs of vervain blue
> Dipt in cold September dew;
> And dash the moisture, chaste and clear
> O'er the ground and through the air –
> Now the place is purged and pure.
> W. Mason (1759)

white horehound

WHITE HOREHOUND (*Marrubium vulgare*). This perennial plant is easily recognized when in bloom, for its little white flowers cluster densely where the leaves join the stem. It is a bushy plant growing about 1 ft (30 cm) high, with wrinkled, woolly leaves facing each other on opposite sides of a woolly stem. It flowers from June to September but will not blossom for the first two years.

The plant can be propagated from seeds grown in spring, the seedlings being thinned out to about 9 in (22 cm) apart when large enough to handle. It is very undemanding as to soil: indeed, it prefers a rather poor soil. It can also be grown by division of the roots, and as the plants age such division is advisable in any case.

The leaves of the white horehound have a variety of uses. A tasty beverage called horehound ale is manufactured from them, and medicinally the herb is used in cough syrups and expectorants and as a mild purgative. A well-known children's medicine was horehound candy, a sweetmeat made of the herb boiled in sugar. In the early part of the 19th century powdered horehound was used as a form of snuff, and the herb is also said to discourage flies in the garden.

lemon balm

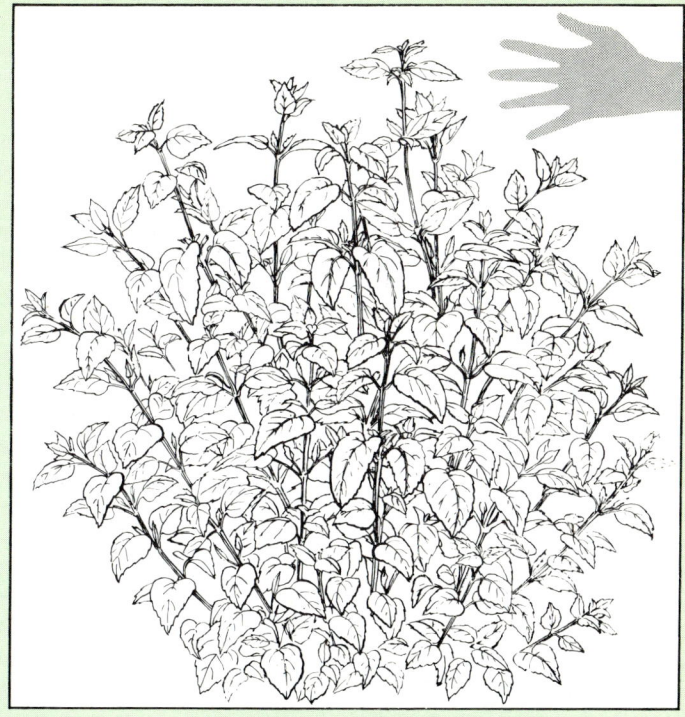

LEMON BALM (*Melissa officinalis*). This is a perennial with invasive creeping roots like those of the mints. It is attractive to bees and forms a bushy plant with hairy, square stems standing up to 3 ft (90 cm) or more high. It has pale green leaves, not unlike those of nettles, which have an aroma of lemons and it is always as much a credit to the flower border for its appearance and aroma as to a herb garden. Its very small white or yellow flowers appear in June and July in the axils of the leaves. In autumn the plant dies down but the roots remain alive and put out new growth the following spring.

Propagation is by shallow sowing outdoors in spring or autumn, or by dividing the roots as with mint. Seedlings should be thinned out to about 1 ft (30 cm) apart. Lemon balm likes well-drained soil and plenty of sun, but little cultivation is called for. The leaves can be gathered and used fresh, as with mint, throughout the summer. If leaves are to be dried they are best picked before flowering takes place.

As may be guessed, its name – a diminutive of balsam – indicates its soothing qualities and it is used in herbal medicine in the form of an infusion to reduce fever. It was long used by bee-keepers inside the hives to stop swarming – an indication of its sweetness – and it gives a refreshing taste to cool summer drinks. It is also used to flavour the liqueur Chartreuse and the perfume Eau de Cologne, and its dried leaves are an ingredient of pot-pourri. Fresh chopped leaves, with their lemon flavour, can be used in salads and sauces.

mint

MINT. There are many varieties of perennial mint but the best-known and most grown are **1** spearmint (*Mentha spicata*), **2** apple mint (*Mentha rotundifolia*), **3** peppermint (*Mentha piperita*) and **4** pennyroyal (*Mentha pulegium*). The common garden mint is **1** spearmint. It grows from creeping roots to between 15 in (37 cm) and 2 ft (60 cm) in height with stiff square stems from which grow its paired aromatic leaves. These are long, narrow, prominently veined and pointed, with serrated edges, and are light green in colour. Its flowers, which appear from July to September, are small and pale purple, and they are followed by tiny brown seeds. The creeping roots spread rapidly.

Because of this slight inconvenience it is advisable, if possible, to confine it by sinking an old bottomless bucket or tin bath and planting inside this area. The sides of the receptacle prevent the roots from spreading and, incidentally, make for a nicely shaped clump of foliage in the garden. Sections of root about 4 in (10 cm) long and with several shoots showing should be planted horizontally at a depth of about 2 in (5 cm) in April and May or in the autumn. Soak the root sections before planting. Every two or three years it is advisable to dig up the clumps and plant out young shoots, thus revivifying the mint. Spearmint likes rich moist soil.

2 Applemint, as its Latin name *rotundifolia* indicates, has rounded leaves quite different from the pointed leaves of the spearmint, although they grow in pairs from the stalk in the same way. It is taller than spearmint and the large leaves are more hairy and a paler green. Its flowers are pale purple, the same as those of spearmint, and appear at the same time.
3 Peppermint, another important member of the family, is not widely grown in gardens but is extensively cultivated commercially to produce oil of peppermint, which is used in many ways. The plant grows to 4 ft (1.2 m) high, has 4-sided stems and bears short-stalked leaves about 2 in (5 cm) long and 1–1½ in (2–3 cm) wide with

Cultivated herbs 65

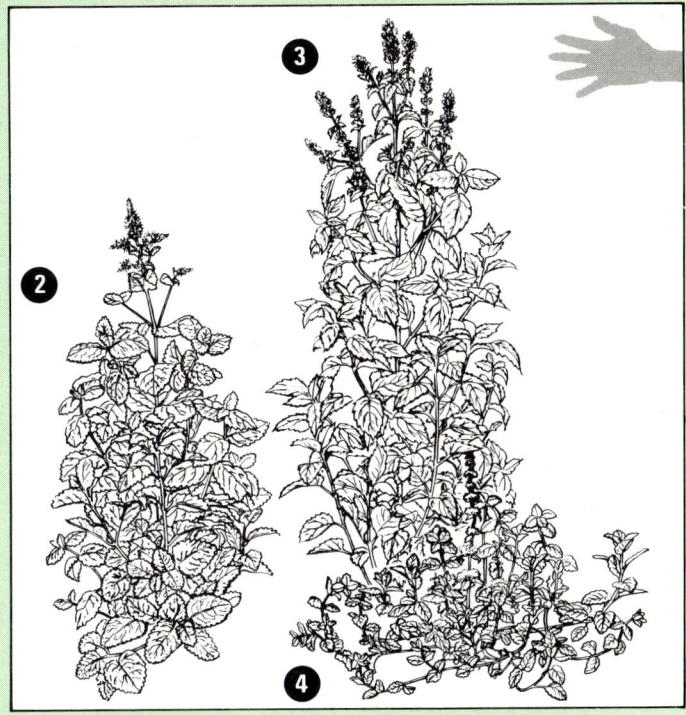

serrated edges. Its small flowers are reddish violet and the whole plant, especially when crushed in any way, has the familiar odour of peppermint.

4 Pennyroyal, although one of the mints, is very different from the other varieties. It is the smallest, the erect variety with its square stems not rising more than 1 ft (30 cm) from the ground. The leaves, nearly round like those of applemint, are greyish green and slightly hairy, and the flowers range from pale blue to a pinkish red.

Spearmint is the culinary herb with which we are all familiar for its characteristic fragrance. Sprigs of it are used to flavour such vegetables as potatoes and peas, and to flavour and garnish fruit drinks. The chopped fresh leaves are made into mint sauce and mint jelly, or used in salads. Applemint is used in much the same way. Peppermint *can* be used in the same way, but its more pronounced flavour may be very much of an acquired taste. An excellent tisane is made from dried peppermint leaves. It is not surprising that the liqueur Crême de Menthe owes its flavour to peppermint, but a little more surprising, perhaps, that two other liqueurs — Bénédictine and Chartreuse — are also flavoured with the mints. Oil of peppermint, whose chief constituent is menthol, has very many commercial uses. It flavours confectionery, toothpaste, toilet preparations etc. It is also used widely in medicine to counteract the effects of dyspepsia, to relieve rheumatism and infections of the throat, and in many other ways. Pennyroyal once had the reputation of driving away fleas. It has a much more pronounced flavour than the other mints and consequently is not used as a culinary herb, although there is an old-fashioned recipe for pennyroyal tea. It is used mainly in herbal medicine.

bergamot

BERGAMOT (*Monarda didyma*). This handsome hardy perennial shrub, standing up to 3 ft (90 cm) high, can with profit be grown in the flower border as well as in the herb garden. Its leaves are mid-green, grow in pairs and are slightly hairy; and its showy tubular flowers, which can range from white to vivid scarlet, grow in whorls on square, grooved stems. The flowers appear from June to September and are so attractive to bees that the plant is sometimes known as bee balm. The whole plant, which is related to mint, has a distinctive fragrance that lingers even when the leaves have fallen.

Wild varieties of bergamot are found near ponds and streams — an indication that it likes a rich, moist soil. In the garden, plants should be about 18 in (45 cm) apart. This is best done by dividing two-year-old plants in March, discarding the centre and planting out the remaining younger sections, about 2 in (5 cm) in width, in a partly shady position. Leaves for drying should be gathered just before the plant flowers; the red flowers are also dried. The stems should be cut down in autumn and the plants should not be left undivided for more than 2 or 3 years.

Bergamot tea is made from either the dried leaves or the flowers of the red bergamot. They should have been carefully dried to keep their colour. Bergamot tea, known in the United States as Oswego tea, was a common beverage there. In Europe it is regarded as a particularly soothing tisane. For medicine its volatile oil is a useful source of thymol, a powerful antiseptic.

sweet cicely

SWEET CICELY (*Myrrhis odorata*). A sturdy, handsome perennial at home in both flower and herb garden, sweet cicely can grow over the years to a height of 5 ft (1.5 m) and nearly as wide. It owes its endearing name not so much to its delicate fragrance as to the sweet, sugary taste of its pale green leaves. These are large, up to 1 ft (30 cm) in length, but nevertheless are delicate and lacy, with white hairs underneath. The stem of the plant is hollow and grooved. Its white flowers appear in May and June, in umbels 3 or 4 in (8–10 cm) in diameter. They are followed by large, dark brown, ribbed seeds. The plant dies down in autumn but puts up new shoots as early as February.

The herb can be grown from seed sown in March or April or from root sections (each containing only one eye) taken after the end of the tap root has been removed. Once established, the plants will usually propagate themselves by self-seeding. Plants should be 1½–2 ft (45–60 cm) apart. They are tough, requiring no special cultivation. Do not allow the flowers to open if you are using the leaves for flavouring.

In the kitchen the chopped leaves of sweet cicely have a variety of uses, mainly because of their sugary taste. They can be used to sweeten tart fruits such as gooseberries and rhubarb; in summer drinks (the herb is one of the flavouring ingredients of the liqueur Chartreuse); and in salads. Some people also eat the roots boiled and served cold with a salad dressing.

myrtle

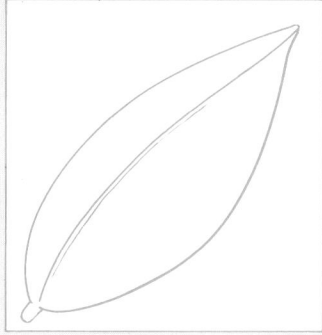

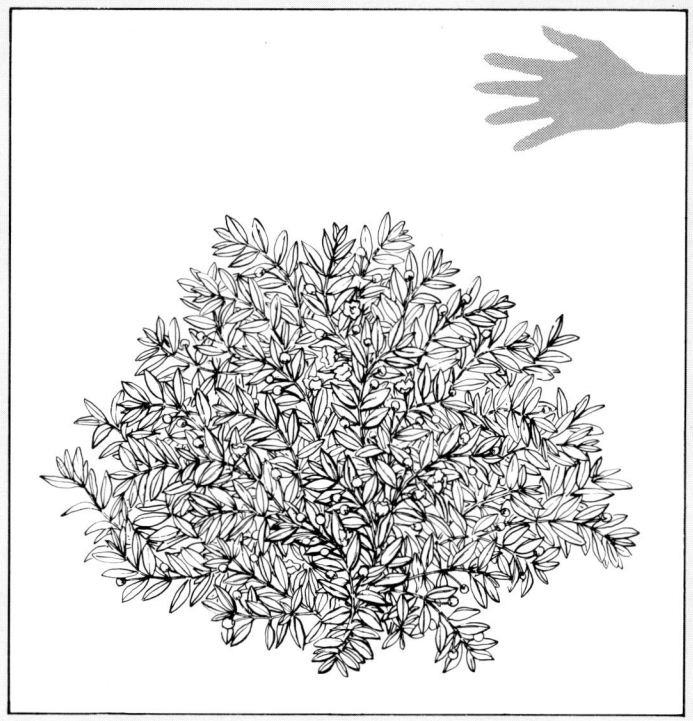

MYRTLE (*Myrtus communis*). There are many varieties of myrtle but this — as its name, the common myrtle, indicates — is the one usually found in herb gardens. It is an evergreen shrub that can grow 8–10 ft (2.5–3 m) high, but as a potted plant can be kept down to 2–3 ft (60–90 cm). It is a pretty shrub, with small, glossy, dark green, pointed leaves that are fragrant when crushed, and bears pinkish white flowers, about 1 in (2 cm) across and with many stamens, from June to August. They grow singly from the leaf axils.

Myrtle is usually grown from heeled cuttings from non-flowering shoots about 3 in (7 cm) long. These are planted in a mixture of peat and sand under glass in June and potted in potting compost. The plants can be planted outdoors during late May, in well-drained soil in a sunny position sheltered from the wind, but this is a decidedly tender plant, and not at all suitable for a chilly or exposed area.

Until quite recently it was not uncommon for a bride to carry a sprig of myrtle in her bouquet of orange blossom and for the bridesmaid to plant the sprig after the ceremony. The custom no doubt arose from the special fragrance of the myrtle's tiny leaves. For the same reason both leaves and flowers are included in pot-pourri.

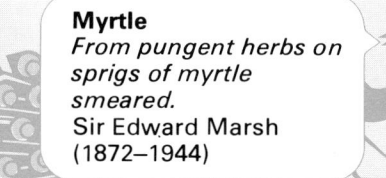

Myrtle
From pungent herbs on sprigs of myrtle smeared.
Sir Edward Marsh (1872–1944)

basil

BASIL (*Ocimum basilicum*). This half-hardy annual has pale green leaves, cool to the touch and usually slightly clove-scented, and grows to a height of between 2 and 3 ft (60–90 cm). The leaves are 1 in (2 cm) long and half that in width and are greyish on the lower side. It is the small oil cells on the underside that make the leaves feel cool. The flowers, which appear in axils of the leaves, are small and white. There are several varieties, identifiable by the shape and scent of the leaves. Sweet basil should not be confused with bush basil, which is much smaller and – although also used for flavouring and in herbal medicine – not so highly regarded as the sweet variety.

In warm climates it can be regarded as a perennial but in Britain it is best sown under glass in the spring and not planted out until all frost danger is past. The distance apart should be about 1 ft (30 cm). Alternatively the herb can be sown where it is to grow in the second half of May and as the seedlings do not like being disturbed this may be preferable. Basil needs well-drained soil in a sunny but sheltered position. Leaves should be cut before the flowers open, but some foliage should be left on to provide a second harvest in the autumn.

The young slightly clove-flavoured leaves are much used in Italian cookery, especially in tomato dishes, but they are also used as an ingredient in many other dishes including chicken and fish and a variety of sauces. The ancients believed that a leaf applied to the sting of a wasp or hornet would suck out the poison. In India the herb has a special significance in Hindu houses where it is regarded as having a protective influence.

> **Basil**
> *O'er it set Sweet Basil,*
> *Which her tears kept*
> *ever wet.*
> Keats (1795–1821) —
> *Isabella or The Pot of Basil*

marjoram

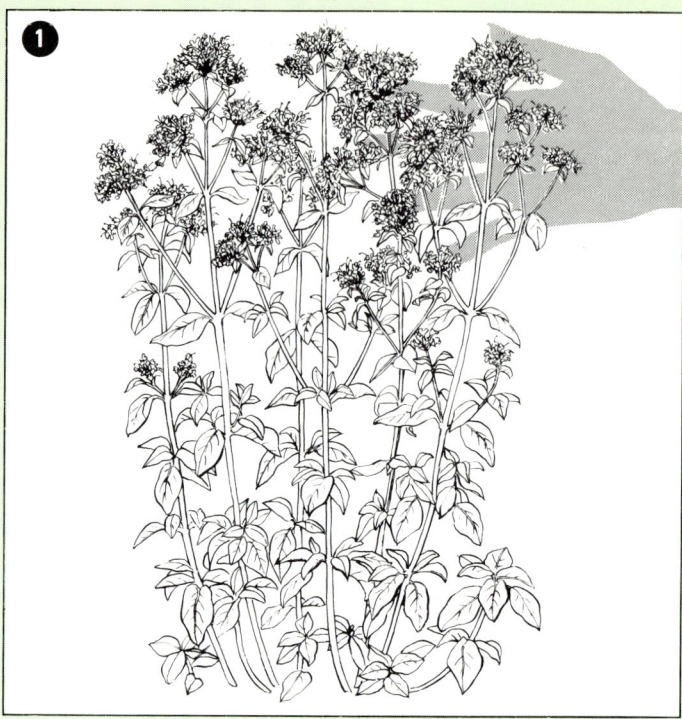

MARJORAM. There are three varieties of marjoram, all perennials: **1** the common marjoram (*Origanum vulgare*), **2** sweet or knotted marjoram (*Origanum marjorana*) and **3** pot marjoram (*Origanum onites*). The dried crumbled leaves of the common marjoram may be sold by your grocer as oregano. Sweet and pot marjoram are the best for the herb garden. Common marjoram grows to a height of 12–18 in (30–45 cm) and has green leaves and small pink-purple flowers in clusters. Sweet or knotted marjoram grows to twice that height, is a bushy, slightly hairy sub-shrub with grey leaves, and has white, pink or purple flowers in close heads like knots. Pot marjoram grows to about 1 ft (30 cm) high, and has square stems, bright green leaves and purple to white flowers. This variety tends to spread.

All the marjorams grow readily in any well-prepared garden exposed to the sun. Seeds can be sown under glass in February or March, hardened off, and transplanted in May to outdoor growing positions. These should be about 9 in (23 cm) apart in rows 12 in (30 cm) apart. If you have no glass, seeds can be sown in shallow drills 9–12 in (23–30 cm) apart in April and seedlings thinned out as above. The seeds are rather long in germination and until the seedlings are of a reasonable size weeding should be done by hand. Once established the plants require little cultivation beyond keeping them free of weeds, and are

Cultivated herbs

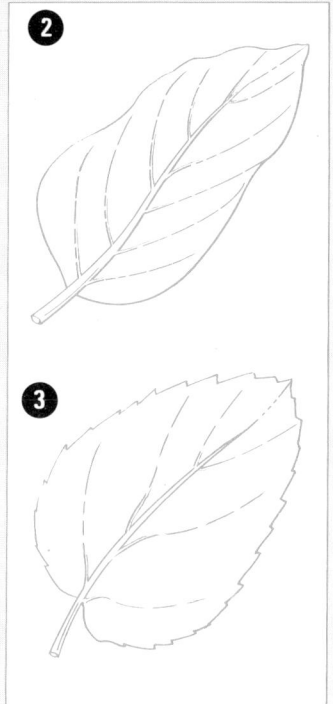

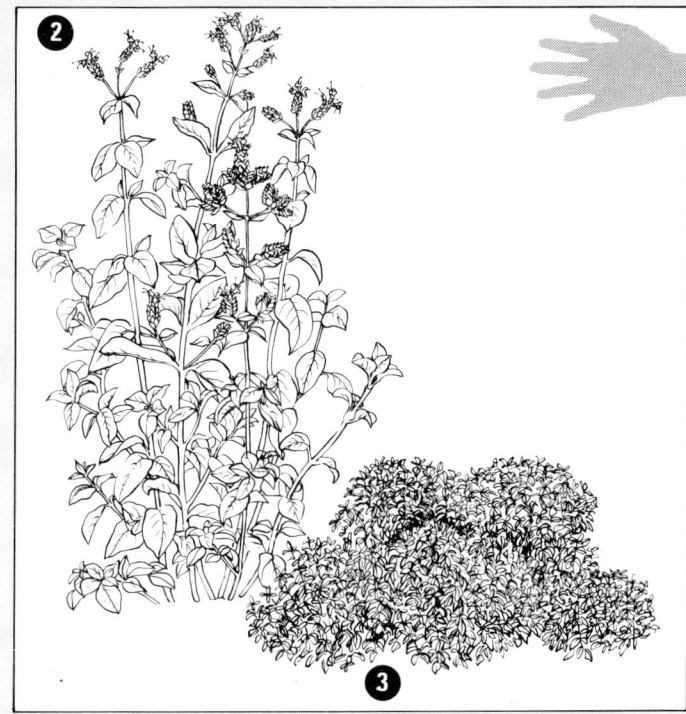

fairly free from disease. Sweet marjoram, though a perennial, will not survive a hard winter, and is best treated as an annual and sown anew each spring. The leaves are best picked for storing just before the plants flower.

As flavouring marjoram is a strong herb for strong dishes. With thyme and sage, dried, it is a traditional ingredient of Mixed Herbs; and fresh with sprigs of thyme and parsley and a bay leaf it makes up a *bouquet garni*. The marjorams, in fact, are favourites among culinary herbs and are used to flavour a very wide variety of dishes. The leaves of common marjoram are used in soups and stews; those of the sweet or knotted marjoram in meat and poultry dishes, omelettes etc; and those of the pot marjoram in stuffings, sausages etc. All are used with such dishes as pizza, spaghetti, tomato dishes etc. Marjoram stores well, keeping its strong flavour. The strong aroma of sweet marjoram makes it particularly suitable for inclusion in pot-pourri. In herbal medicine marjoram is sometimes used as a hot fomentation for swellings and rheumatism.

Marjoram

Lafeu: 'Twas a good lady, 'twas a good lady: we may pick a thousand salads ere we light on such another herb.
Clown: Indeed, sir, she was the sweetest Marjoram of the salad or rather the Herb of Grace.
Lafeu: They are not salad herbs, you knave, they are nose herbs.
Clown: I am no great Nebuchadnezzar, sir, I have not much skill in grass.

Shakespeare (1564–1616) — *All's Well that Ends Well*

anise

ANISE (*Pimpinella anisum*). This delicate-looking annual grows to about 18 in (45 cm) high. It has bright green feathery leaves and looks not unlike a slim celery plant. Its creamy white flowers appear in umbels 2 in (5 cm) across in July. It is a very ancient herb, which came originally from the Middle East and is mentioned in the Bible: 'Ye pay tithe of mint and anise and cumin' (*Matthew* XXI''). Although grown mainly for commercial reasons, it is a familiar inhabitant of the herb garden.

Not surprisingly, considering its origins, it prefers dry, light soil exposed to plenty of sun. It may be sown where it is to grow, in shallow drills, and the seedlings thinned out to about 1 ft (30 cm) apart. Or it can be grown in pots under glass and planted out in May. Keep free from weeds. It is the seeds that are used and a good warm summer is required to bring them to maturity. When matured they can be shaken from the stem and dried and stored.

The flavour of anise — or aniseed — is used not only in the manufacture of sweets but also, in cough lozenges, to relieve catarrh. It is also used as a remedy for digestive disorders, and is a familiar flavouring in liqueurs and cordials. Only occasionally is it used in the kitchen and then sparingly, usually in fish dishes.

Anise
*For the dropsie fill an old cock with Polypody and Aniseed and seethe him well, and drink the broth.
Langham (1683) —
Garden Health*

purslane

PURSLANE (*Portulaca oleracea*). This highly decorative herb is a very low-growing annual – only about 6 in (15 cm) high – with smooth, succulent, red stems and either dark green or golden oblong leaves that grow in profusion. Its flowers are small and yellow and appear in June or July. They are unusual in that they open for only a very short time each day, usually about midday.

The golden purslane (known as *Portulaca sativa*) is not as hardy as the green. Both can be grown from seed in the open from May onwards (or in hotbeds for planting out in May) and mature quickly in warm weather. They prefer a light soil and a warm but shady position, but also like moisture and should be watered regularly in dry weather. Like lettuces they should be sown at intervals to ensure a succession. Cut the plants low when you are gathering the leaves, to encourage further growth. Keep free from weeds.

The leaves of purslane, whether green or golden, can be used in salads just like lettuce leaves and are particularly succulent. At one time the herb was popular in medicine and was believed to counteract harmful magic. Its juice was used as a lotion for sore gums, and a concoction of the seeds in wine was used against worms in children. Today its use is confined to the kitchen, either in salads or as a flavouring for soup.

rose

ROSES (*Rosaceae*). More usually found in the flower garden, roses nevertheless have their uses in the kitchen, in medicine and in perfumery, and thus would not be out of place in the herb garden. A description is almost superfluous, roses being familiar perennial shrubs of many varieties, their common features being their strong, angular, thorned stems bearing oval toothed leaves and their rich and colourful flowering habits. Their flowers, which appear from June onwards, are of many different colours and sizes, and consist of tightly packed, often exceptionally fragrant, petals that open out as the plant matures, falling in the autumn to leave a plump fruit or hip.

Roses are often propagated from cuttings taken in autumn. These should be about 9–12 in (23–30 cm) long and should have a heel. Except for 2 or 3 at the top, leaves should be removed; the root is then dipped in a hormone rooting powder and the cutting planted in a sheltered part of the garden. With luck the young rose should be ready to plant out in the growing position the following autumn. Another method of propagation is by grafting a growth bud on the rootstock of a wild rose. Roses like rich, well-manured soil. Suckers should be cut off at the roots and the trees kept regularly pruned.

The favourite rose for use in the house or in perfumery is the red damask rose, which is heavily scented. Its petals are used in pot-pourri (as are the petals of many other roses, although red ones are preferable). Attar of roses – the essential oil distilled from the petals, and the basis of many perfumes – is made in many countries commercially. Rose-water is used not only in cooking but in medicine to sweeten disagreeable flavours. Rose hips are used to make rose hip syrup, rich in Vitamin C.

rosemary

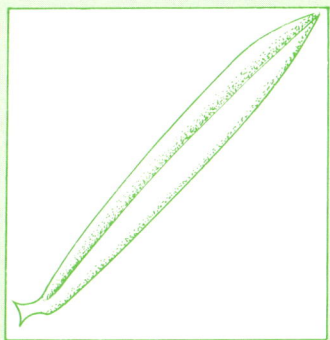

ROSEMARY (*Rosmarinus officinalis*). This attractive evergreen flowering shrub is sufficiently decorative to earn its place in the flower garden as well as supplying a fragrant herb for the kitchen. It grows to a height of 5 ft (1.5 m) or more. The leaves, very narrow and about 1 in (2 cm) long, are a shiny dark green on top and a much paler green, almost grey, underneath. They are aromatic, faintly reminiscent of camphor in smell, and need only to be touched to leave their fragrance on the hand. The herb bears blue flowers in March or April and then in smaller numbers throughout the summer.

Rosemary can be grown from seeds (although germination is undependable) or cuttings and is happy in average well-drained soil in a sunny, sheltered position. Sowing in the open should be in April in shallow drills 6 in (15 cm) apart, the seedlings being transplanted to 6 in (15 cm) apart into a nursery bed when about 3 in (7 cm) high. Eventually they should be planted out 3 ft (90 cm) apart. Heeled cuttings, about 6 in (15 cm) long, can be taken in June after the plants have flowered and put about 4 in (10 cm) deep in shaded sandy soil. They should be ready for transplanting to their permanent home in the autumn. The leaves are used either fresh or dried.

The herb has many uses in cooking, medicine and cosmetics. The oil from its flower tops is used in Eau de Cologne and in shampoos, hair lotions and bath essence. Traditionally rosemary was a love token, and formed part of a bride's wreath. Its leaves and flowers make rosemary tea, which is said to be good for headaches and colds. But its main popular use is in cooking, and its highly individual taste is excellent with highly flavoured dishes such as venison or pheasant and a wide variety of other dishes.

sorrel

SORREL. There are two main varieties of this perennial herb: French sorrel (*Rumex scutatus*) and **(a)** the common or English variety (*Rumex acetosa*). Both grow to a height of 18 in (45 cm) but the French variety is the more popular in the herb garden because its leaves are less acid. Its leaves are oblong, the upper ones being directly attached to the stalk: they sometimes turn red. In June and July the plant forms spikes of greenish red flowers, which are followed by brown, shiny seeds.

Sorrel can be sown in the open in late March in a sunny but sheltered position with a rich soil; the English variety prefers a moist soil, the French variety a dry one. Sow fairly thinly in shallow drills, and when the seedlings are big enough to handle thin out to about 1 ft (30 cm) apart. Cut back in July to encourage the growth of young leaves. It is a good plan to stagger this cutting back to ensure a steady supply of young leaves. In autumn the roots may be divided and the sections planted out 1 ft (30 cm) apart.

The leaves of both varieties can be used in salads, but because they are rather acid in taste (the French variety less so) they are usually mixed with lettuce leaves. Sorrel is also used in soups and can be cooked and eaten like spinach. In the past it was made into a well-known 'green sauce', incidentally one of its present-day country names. In herbal medicine the acidic sorrel has the reputation of being helpful in cases of scurvy and jaundice.

rue

RUE (*Ruta graveolens*). This is a small hardy evergreen shrub, useful for decoration in the garden but characterized by a rather objectionable smell. Rue can have a bad influence on certain herbs if it is grown next to them, especially sweet basil. It grows to a height of between 2 and 3 ft (60–90 cm) and has bluish green, almost fern-like leaves. One variety, Jackman's Blue, is shorter and has much more pronounced blue leaves. The shrub flourishes from June to September, the rather insignificant yellow blooms appearing in clusters at the end of the stems.

Rue can be grown from seeds or from cuttings. The seeds are sown in spring, broadcast, and the seedlings eventually thinned out to about 18 in (45 cm) apart. Cuttings, planted in spring, are best brought on in shade before being planted out the same distance apart as the seedlings. The shrub prefers a dry, rather sheltered situation and requires little cultivation. Cutting back to the old wood in April encourages bushy growth; it also helps to pinch out the growing tips.

The leaves of rue, finely chopped, are sometimes used in salads, but their bitter flavour is something of an acquired taste. It was one of the ancient strewing herbs, perhaps because of its reputation for killing fleas and as an antiseptic. A tisane may be made from its leaves, but is very bitter and calls for a great deal of sweetening.

Rue
If a man be anointed with the juice of Rue, the poison of wolf's bane, mushrooms, or todestooles, the biting of serpents, stinging of scorpions, spiders, bees, hornets and wasps will not hurt him.
Gerard – (1597)

sage

SAGE (*Salvia officinalis*). It is very easy to recognize this small hardy evergreen shrub. It grows to about 2 ft (60 cm) in height, with rather woody four-sided stems, and its leaves, set in pairs and about 1½–2 in (3–5 cm) long and 1 in (2 cm) wide, are grey-green in colour, crinkly in appearance and highly aromatic, especially when crushed. In mid-summer the plant produces violet-blue flowers, two-lipped and about 1 in (2 cm) long, which are very attractive to bees. There are many varieties, some gold or purple, which are handsome as well as useful. Sage is a perennial, but after 4 or 5 years the plants get leggy, and begin to show their age, and they should then be replaced.

It is not choosy where it grows but likes well-drained light soil in a warm, slightly shaded position. Sage is propagated from seeds or by cuttings. Seeds can be sown in boxes under glass in March or in the open a month later. When large enough to handle, plant the seedlings out in a nursery bed and later where they are to grow 15 in (37 cm) apart. The more certain way is propagation by cuttings with heels taken in September and planted in peat and sand, then transferred to potting compost in a cold frame where they can spend the winter. Sage bushes should be fed in late autumn with old manure or well-rotted compost.

Sage leaves can be used in the kitchen either fresh or dried. Drying is more difficult than with most herbs because of the toughness of the leaves. Used fresh the leaves are large and strong enough to be wrapped around pieces of meat and fish, and sage is valued for counteracting rich and greasy foods such as goose or duck. Sage and onion stuffing is eaten with roast pork for the same reason. Its Latin name *Salvia* relates to health and it has a long history of use in herbal medicine.

elder

ELDER (*Sambucus nigra*). This is not one of the tidy little plants in the border of your herb garden, but a shrub or small tree growing as high as 15 ft (4.5 m) and equally wide. But you may well find space for one in your hedge and profit from it. There are many species but this is the most familiar in Europe. The trunk is soft and woody and the straight stems have a pithy interior (hollowed out by country lads to make peashooters, whistles etc). The leaf stems have 2 or 3 pairs of rich, dark green, pointed leaves facing each other and a terminal leaf. In June the tree carries large umbels, up to 6 in (15 cm) across, of creamy white flowers, which are followed in September by shiny black or dark violet berries.

Elders like damp, rich soil, preferably in a sunny position, but are not averse to being crowded, which is why they flourish in hedges. They can be propagated by cuttings of woody shoots taken in the autumn and brought on in a nursery bed for a year before being planted out in their permanent positions. Then they will look after themselves, but pruning in early spring (before annual growth starts) or in late autumn will help to keep the tree under control.

Both flowers and berries can be used in many different ways. The dried flowers can be used to make elderflower tea, or mixed with lime and camomile to produce a strong-flavoured tisane. They can also be made into a summer drink. The dried berries can be used as a substitute for currants, and elderberry wine, potent and comforting, has been a staple product of home wine-making for centuries. A hot cordial made from the berries is used in herbal medicine to alleviate catarrh and as a remedy for bronchitis and the bark is used as a purgative. In the field of cosmetics elderflower water is used as a lotion for the skin.

salad burnet

SALAD BURNET (*Poterium sanguisorba*). This perennial herb makes an attractive border, its bright green foliage putting up a brave show in the winter months. It grows to between 12 and 15 in (30–37 cm) high and has very small, close-growing pinnate leaves, 8 or 9 pairs to a stem, which are less than ½ in (1 cm) long. The flower stems rise well above the plant and produce at their tips first small, round clusters (not unlike raspberries) of pale mauve balls, then green flowers that later turn reddish.

Although it is a perennial many gardeners prefer to treat salad burnet as an annual, especially as it will seed itself if allowed to. It can be sown in April in ½ in (1 cm) drills 1 ft (30 cm) apart and thinned out when ready to handle to about 9 in (23 cm) apart. It is tough and grows in almost any soil, with a slight preference for chalk, but requires little cultivation beyond watering in dry weather. Plants may be propagated by dividing the roots in the autumn.

The leaves of salad burnet taste and smell slightly of cucumber (although they are not related) and consequently are a useful ingredient of salads. They are also used to garnish and flavour fruit drinks and as an ingredient for mild soups. Salad burnet was long regarded as a useful astringent for congealing the blood in the treatment of wounds.

Burnet
But those which perfume the air most delightfully, . . . being trodden upon and crushed, are three: that is, burnet, wild thyme, and water mints. Therefore you are to set whole alleys of them, to have the pleasure, when you walk or tread
Bacon (1561–1626)

savory

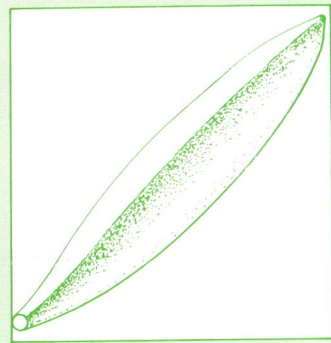

SAVORY. There are many varieties of this well-named herb but two are chiefly grown, the annual summer savory (*Satureia hortensis*) and the perennial winter savory (*Satureia montana*). Both are sub-shrubs growing to about 1 ft (30 cm) high but they are otherwise quite different in appearance. Summer savory, the more popular, has slender, dark green leaves on opposite sides of erect square stems, slightly pink in colour and hairy. It has small lilac or purple flowers growing from the leaf axils and these appear from July to September. Winter savory spreads more and has a more woody stem, and the leaves are small and a greyish green. The flowers can be light purple, pink or white.

Both varieties can be grown from seed. Sow in a cold frame in March or outdoors in April, in shallow drills 1 ft (30 cm) apart, thinning out to about 8 in (20 cm) apart. They prefer light, well-drained soil in a sunny position. They can also be propagated by division in spring or from cuttings taken in May. These are brought on in peat and sand in a cold frame, then potted singly and kept in the cold frame until the following spring. Once established little cultivation is required.

The leaves of both varieties can be used fresh or dried, but winter savory is usually available fresh throughout the year. If you are using it for drying, harvest summer savory in August. The leaves of winter savory have a coarser flavour than those of summer savory; many prefer the latter in the kitchen. They have a strong peppery, spicy flavour and are used frequently with all types of beans, and in soups (especially those of the vegetable variety) and many meat and cheese dishes. The leaves are also often used as an ingredient of pot-pourri. Savory tea can also be made.

comfrey

COMFREY (*Symphytum officinale*). This herb is a member of the borage family. It has a strong, hollow stem, and grows to about 3 ft (90 cm) in height; the lower part of its leaves runs along the stem before branching out. As in borage, the lower leaves are very large and all the leaves, mid-green in colour, are hairy. In early summer its delicate sprays of small bell-shaped flowers may be either creamy yellow or lavender. They are followed by small black nuts, in fours.

Be careful with comfrey in the herb garden. Once established its brittle roots take a firm grip on the garden and even a tiny portion, broken off, will produce a new plant. It is a good plan to grow it in a bucket or container of some sort, to prevent this. The herb grows almost anywhere except in very dry soil, but it has a preference for shady, damp places. It is usually grown from root sections planted about 2½ ft (75 cm) apart, but can be grown from seed sown in spring or autumn. It is fairly free from pests and diseases and requires no special cultivation.

Comfrey has many country names and three of them — bruisewort, knitbone and boneset — are a clear reminder of its traditional use in treating wounds and broken bones. This may be due in part to its high mucilage content and the leaves have long been used to make poultices. An infusion of comfrey leaves is said to be useful against colds and ulcers, and the root has been used as an ingredient for a coffee substitute.

tansy

TANSY (*Tanacetum vulgare*). A handsome herb, a credit to the flower garden as well as to the herb garden, tansy is a hardy perennial that also grows wild in hedgerows. It has erect stems, slightly pink, which grow to a height of about 3 ft (90 cm). It has darkish green leaves, deeply indented, which grow alternately and have a rather fern-like appearance. It is easily recognized by its characteristic tiny, hard, dull-yellow flowers tightly packed in solid flat clusters about 2 in (5 cm) in diameter, which smell faintly of camphor and appear in July.

As its profusion in the wild suggests, tansy is easy to cultivate, and flourishes in almost any soil. It can be propagated by dividing existing roots in spring or autumn and planting them 1 ft (30 cm) or more apart. The tansy's roots, which grow close to the surface, are inclined to run wild and to take over the ground if not kept under control. Tansy looks after itself and no special cultivation is required.

Tansy has a reputation for keeping away flies, and this was probably the reason why in olden days it was used as one of the strewing herbs, ie those scattered on the floors of houses and public places. It has no particular culinary virtues, although at one time tansy cakes and bread were made from its leaves, usually at Easter time. Medicinally it has been used as a vermicide for children and as a hot fomentation against rheumatism. If hung in bunches in the dark the flowers dry exceedingly well and are useful contributors to floral decorations of dried flowers.

costmary

COSTMARY (*Tanacetum balsamita*). Also known as alecost, this perennial herb is closely related to the tansy and like it has a rapidly spreading root system just below the soil surface. But its leaves are different, being broad and whole rather than feathery. It grows to a height of up to 3 ft (90 cm) with clusters of yellow flowers appearing in August. It is a straggly and not particularly attractive plant, even when in flower. The whole plant has a pleasant aroma.

Costmary grows vigorously but will not flower if grown in shade. It likes a sunny, dry position and requires little cultivation. It is propagated by the division of roots, sections being planted about 2 ft (60 cm) apart. This can be done in either spring or autumn. Because of the rapid growth of the root system the roots need dividing every 2 or 3 years.

In olden days costmary was one of the strewing herbs, and it was used medicinally as an antiseptic and against dysentery. Crushed, the leaves relieve pain if rubbed on bee stings. As its old name of alecost suggests, it was used for beer-making in the Middle Ages.

> **Costmary**
> *The conserve made with leaves of Costmaria and sugar doth warm and dry the braine and openeth the stoppings of the same; stoppeth all catarrhs, rheumes and distillations, taken in the quantitie of a beane.*
> Gerard (1545–1612)

# thyme

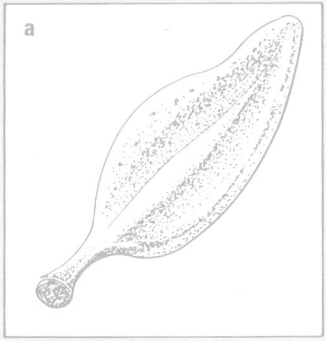

THYME. Common thyme (*Thymus vulgaris*) is one of the most popular garden herbs (a) and better known than its relative lemon thyme (*Thymus citriodorus*). They are both small hardy evergreen shrubs, the common thyme growing to about 8 in (20 cm) high or less and the lemon variety to about 1 ft (30 cm). The common thyme has small, narrow, dark green, aromatic leaves on hard, woody stems and the plant bears very small pinkish flowers between June and August. Lemon thyme is similar in appearance, but its leaves are broader and lemon-scented and the flowers slightly darker and larger. Some varieties have golden or variegated leaves.

Both varieties may be grown from seeds or from cuttings. They like a well-drained chalky soil in a sunny position. Seeds should be sown in a cold frame, and the established seedlings transplanted into pots and planted out 1 ft (30 cm) apart in September. The plants tend to become woody in time and should be replaced every 3 or 4 years; this can be done from cuttings. The beds should be kept well weeded and well watered. Plants should be cut back in autumn and may need some protection (eg leaf mould) against frost, particularly lemon thyme. Leaves for drying should be harvested before flowering finishes.

With marjoram, parsley and a bay leaf, a sprig of common thyme makes up the traditional *bouquet garni* used for flavouring stews, soups and sauces. It is a strongly flavoured aromatic herb and should be used sparingly with other herbs: it may be included with almost any meat or fish dish and with a great many vegetables. Lemon thyme, with its additional lemon flavour, is rather more delicate. Thyme is one of the herbs used to flavour the liqueur Bénédictine. The important antiseptic thymol is extracted from its volatile oil, and essence of thyme is used in the manufacture of cosmetics.

nasturtium

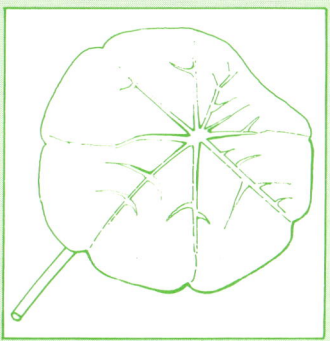

NASTURTIUM (*Tropaeolum majus*). Often grown in the flower garden, the nasturtium is a trailing or climbing annual characterized by its pale green, kidney-shaped leaves and its vivid flowers. These grow in profusion in mid-summer, are shaped like a mediaeval monk's cowl and are bright orange or yellow in colour. The flat leaves have a pungent flavour. The flowers are followed by large, pale green seeds. In the herb garden it is more convenient to plant compact varieties.

Nasturtiums like rather light soil in an open, sunny position. They are grown from seed, which is sown where the plants are to remain, but they are prolific self-seeders and once they are established it is mostly a matter of thinning out. They are naturally strong growers and no special attention is required.

The leaves have a very high Vitamin C content, but need to be used with some caution because of their hot flavour. They can be used in salads, added to cream cheese, even made into sandwiches between sliced bread and butter. The dried seeds can be ground and used as a substitute for pepper or, if pickled when young, as a substitute for capers.

Better is a dinner of herbs where love is, than a stalled ox and hatred therewith.
Proverbs XV 17

valerian

VALERIAN (*Valeriana officinalis*). This perennial herb can grow as high as 5 ft (1.5 m), although it is usually about 3–4 ft (90–120 cm). Valerians grow from an upright rhizome, with sturdy round, grooved and hairy stems. These carry on the lower part stalked pinnate leaves and, higher up, leaflets that are deeply indented. The flowers, which bloom from June to September, are small and pink, and grow in loose clusters. The aroma exuded by the plant is not very agreeable.

Valerian is undemanding, flourishing in most soils but preferring a damp position. It can be grown from seed sown outdoors in April. The seeds should not be covered, simply pressed in, and because germination is slow and not always reliable, sow generously and mark the place clearly. When the seedlings are ready to handle, plant them out about 1 ft (30 cm) apart, in rows 2 ft (60 cm) apart. It may be 2 years or more before the plant flowers. Valerian can also be propagated by dividing the roots, which can be lifted in the autumn of the second year of growth. If the flowering points are stopped when they appear, the rhizomes will improve.

The dull brown rhizomes contain a powerful volatile oil that has sedative qualities. They should be cut before drying, as this reduces their offensive odour. Cut in small pieces and steeped in water they make a tea that has a tranquillizing and soporific effect.

*Then springen herbes grete and smale,
The licoris and the setewale.*
Chaucer (1340–1400)

corn salad

CORN SALAD (*Valerianella olitoria*). This low-growing annual herb looks somewhat like a lettuce, and is, indeed, sometimes known as lambs' lettuce. It grows to a height of between 6 and 12 in (15–30 cm) and its bright green, spoon-shaped leaves grow in a clump rather like a loose small-leaved lettuce. The tiny flowers, which appear in high summer, are whitish green, almost colourless.

Corn salad can be grown from seed, sown thinly in shallow drills about 8 in (20 cm) apart, from autumn until early spring. Sowing can be made every other week to ensure succession. Germination and growth are quick and as the leaves are eaten while young there is no need to thin out seedlings except to eat them. The plant likes a sheltered but sunny position in well-manured soil. Pull the plants whole while still young and cut off the roots.

The great virtue of corn salad lies in its growth throughout the winter, thus providing a fresh salad in place of lettuce.

> *Rare things please us: so there is greater relish for the earliest fruit of the season, and roses in winter command a high price.*
> Martial (AD 40–104)

mullein

MULLEIN (*Verbascum thapsus*). One of the most handsome plants in any garden, mullein or verbascum can grow as high as 8 ft (2.4 m), although 4–5 ft (1.2–1.5 m) is a more normal height. It is a biennial with a single round stem, along which grow alternating spearhead-shaped leaves that are pale green and covered with fine white hairs or down. Those at the base can be 8 in (20 cm) or more long and 3 in (7.5 cm) wide. The plant blooms in July and August, and its yellow, stalkless flowers with orange stamens are very attractive to bees. Unfortunately it is also very attractive to other insects, including aphids, caterpillars and other pests.

Because of their height, the plants should be sheltered from the wind, although they like a sunny position. They prefer a chalky soil but will grow almost anywhere and require no cultivation as such. They can be grown from seed sown in a nursery bed in spring: the seedlings are planted out in late August or September where they are to grow, up to 2 ft (60 cm) apart. These should flower in the following summer. Once established, the plants perpetuate themselves by self-seeding. The flowers should be picked regularly as they open.

It is the flowers of the plant that are used, mainly in herbal medicine and to make a yellow dye. They are used to relieve bronchial catarrh and coughs.

Mullein
The whole toppe, with its pleasant yellow floures, sheweth like a wax candle or taper cunningly wrought. (1578) — The Niewe Herbal

violet

VIOLET (*Viola odorata*). Perhaps more at home in the flower bed than in the herb garden, the sweet violet is highly decorative to both. It is a perennial growing to about 5 in (12 cm), with medium to dark green heart-shaped leaves and purple flowers. These may show as early as February and can go on for about 2 months. Sometimes the plant blooms again in autumn, but with much smaller flowers. The flowers have a fragrant scent. The plant spreads by means of runners from which new plants grow directly.

The sweet violet likes some shade but must have some sun too. It prefers a deep, sandy soil that has been well dug. Rooted runners should be planted in spring about 1 ft (30 cm) apart and the soil well moistened. It is helpful to protect the very young plants from the sun and they must be kept well watered in dry weather. Watch for signs of red spider, ie yellowing leaves, and keep free from weeds.

Crystallized violets – the flowers in sugar – are attractive as decorations on confectionery, and quite easy to prepare, although the drying of the flowers calls for great care. Both leaves and flowers are rich in Vitamin C and can be used in salads, and the flowers are made into a syrup used as a laxative. They are also used for colouring material and in the manufacture of perfumery and cosmetic preparations.

chapter three
wild herbs

HERB	BOTANICAL NAME	OTHER NAMES	🫗	🫙	✴	PAGES
Betony	Stachys betonica	bishopswort		🫙		115
Burdock	Arctium lappa	beggar's buttons love leaves clot-bur	🫗	🫙		101
Chickweed	Stellaria media	starweed passerina	🫗	🫙		113
Cowslip	Primula veris	herb Peter Our Lady's keys fairy cups	🫗	🫙		112
Dandelion	Taraxacum officinale	priest's crown swine's snout	🫗			116
Deadly nightshade	Atropa belladonna	belladonna devil's cherries devil's herb	☠	🫙		105
Foxglove	Digitalis purpurea	fairy thimbles dead men's bells witches' gloves	☠	🫙		106
Henbane	Hyoscyamus niger	hog's bean Jupiter's bean	☠	🫙		109
Lady's mantle	Alchemilla vulgaris	lion's foot		🫙		100
Meadowsweet	Spiraea ulmaria	queen of the meadow bridewort	🫗	🫙		114
Mugwort	Artemisia vulgaris	St John's plant	🫗			103
Nettles	Urtica dioica Urtica urens	stinging nettle	🫗	🫙		117
Poppies	Papaver rhoeas Papaver somniferum	red poppy corn poppy white poppy opium poppy	🫗 ☠	🫙 🫙		110
Willow-herb	Epilobium angustifolium	rosebay blood vine purple rocket	🫗	🫙		107
Witch hazel	Hamamelis virginiana	spotted alder snapping hazelnut		🫙		108
Woodruff	Asperula odorata	sweet woodruff	🫗		✴	104
Wormwood	Artemisia absinthium		🫗	🫙		102

Wild herbs 97

left
HERB
This is the name by which the herb is most often known in common speech.
BOTANICAL NAME
The botanical name may have changed over the years, but is internationally known.
OTHER NAMES
These are often very local names for each herb, and one plant may have several.
COOKING
This symbol shows that the herb can be used in recipes to flavour foods.
SCENT
This sign shows the herbs that are used for scented toilet preparations.
POMANDERS
This shows that the herb is suitable for inclusion in pomanders and pot-pourri.
POISON
This symbol shows which herbs are highly poisonous, and *must not* be eaten.

right
Arrangement of chapter

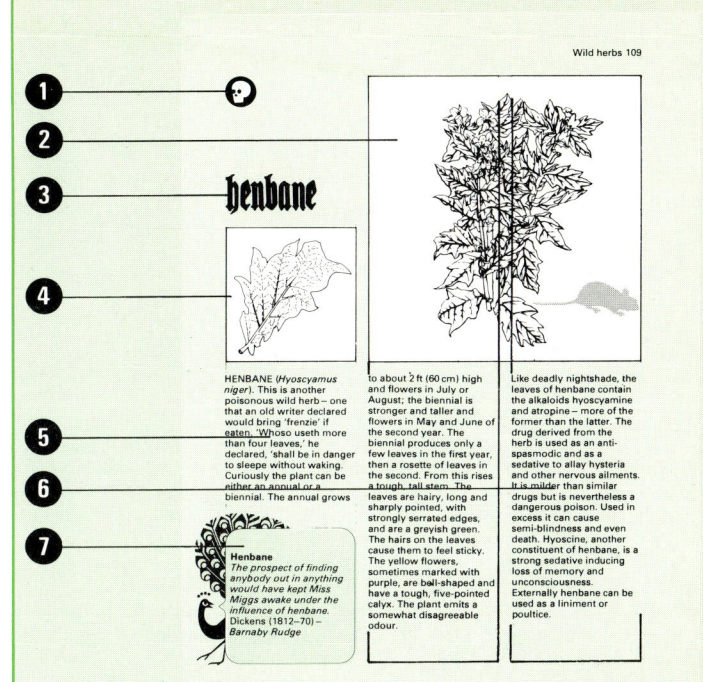

Wild herbs 109

henbane

HENBANE (*Hyoscyamus niger*). This is another poisonous wild herb – one that an old writer declared would bring 'frenzie' if eaten. 'Whoso useth more than four leaves,' he declared, 'shall be in danger to sleepe without waking. Curiously the plant can be either an annual or a biennial. The annual grows to about 2 ft (60 cm) high and flowers in July or August; the biennial is stronger and taller and flowers in May and June of the second year. The biennial produces only a few leaves in the first year, then a rosette of leaves in the second. From this rises a tough, tall stem. The leaves are hairy, long and sharply pointed, with strongly serrated edges, and are a greyish green. The hairs on the leaves cause them to feel sticky. The yellow flowers, sometimes marked with purple, are bell-shaped and have a tough, five-pointed calyx. The plant emits a somewhat disagreeable odour.

Like deadly nightshade, the leaves of henbane contain the alkaloids hyoscyamine and atropine – more of the former than the latter. The drug derived from the herb is used as an antispasmodic and as a sedative to allay hysteria and other nervous ailments. It is milder than similar drugs but is nevertheless a dangerous poison. Used in excess it can cause semi-blindness and even death. Hyoscine, another constituent of henbane, is a strong sedative inducing loss of memory and unconsciousness. Externally henbane can be used as a liniment or poultice.

Henbane
The prospect of finding anybody out in anything would have kept Miss Miggs awake under the influence of henbane.
Dickens (1812–70) – *Barnaby Rudge*

1
A skull symbol in the top left-hand corner of the page means that the herb is poisonous, and should be handled very carefully.
2
The large drawing on the right-hand side of each page shows an example of the whole plant. Plants vary in size slightly, according to the conditions under which they grow, but the little fieldmouse gives an idea of the scale. The mouse measures about 6 in (15 cm) from its nose to the tip of its tail.
3
Each of the herbs is introduced by the common name by which it is most generally known in Britain.
4
A single leaf of each separate species has been drawn, to help you to identify the plants with certainty, but this drawing is not to scale.
5
The first part of the text gives a full description of each plant, including its leaves, stem and flowers, and also the time of year when it usually blooms and the sort of area where it may be found growing wild.
6
The second part of the text describes the uses of the various parts of the herb; some of these are still practicable now, but others are outmoded.
7
Occasional quotations from writers throughout the ages show how herbs have always exerted a strong fascination over men's minds, and also enriched their comfort.

98 Chapter three

where they grow

Wild herbs flourish in a variety of surroundings. Some are at home in damp conditions, beside streams; others prefer the open spaces, either fairly lush fields and meadows or dry and apparently inhospitable wastelands; many species push up in hedgerows or ditches; and still others enjoy the shade of woods and copses. This illustration shows the preferred conditions of the best-known common wild herbs. Some of them, such as burdock and betony, are tolerant and will grow in various types of countryside.

Woods and copses
Betony
Deadly nightshade
Foxglove
Witch hazel
Woodruff

Hedgerows and ditches
Betony
Burdock
Chickweed
Deadly nightshade
Foxglove

Henbane
Mugwort
Nettle
Witch hazel
Wormwood

Wild herbs

FLOWERING TIME Herb and colour	Apr	May	June	July	Aug	Sept
Betony *red purple*				❋	❋	
Burdock *purplish*				❋	❋	
Chickweed *white*	❋	❋	❋	❋	❋	❋
Cowslip *yellow*	❋	❋				
Dandelion *yellow*	❋	❋	❋	❋	❋	❋
Deadly nightshade *purple*			❋	❋		
Foxglove *purple, white*			❋	❋		
Henbane *yellow*		❋	❋	❋	❋	
Lady's mantle *green*			❋	❋	❋	
Meadowsweet *yellowish white*			❋	❋	❋	
Mugwort *reddish, pale yellow*				❋	❋	❋
Nettle *pale green*				❋	❋	
Poppy *red, white*			❋	❋	❋	
Willow-herb *purple*				❋		
Witch hazel *yellow*						❋
Woodruff *white*		❋	❋			
Wormwood *yellow*				❋	❋	❋

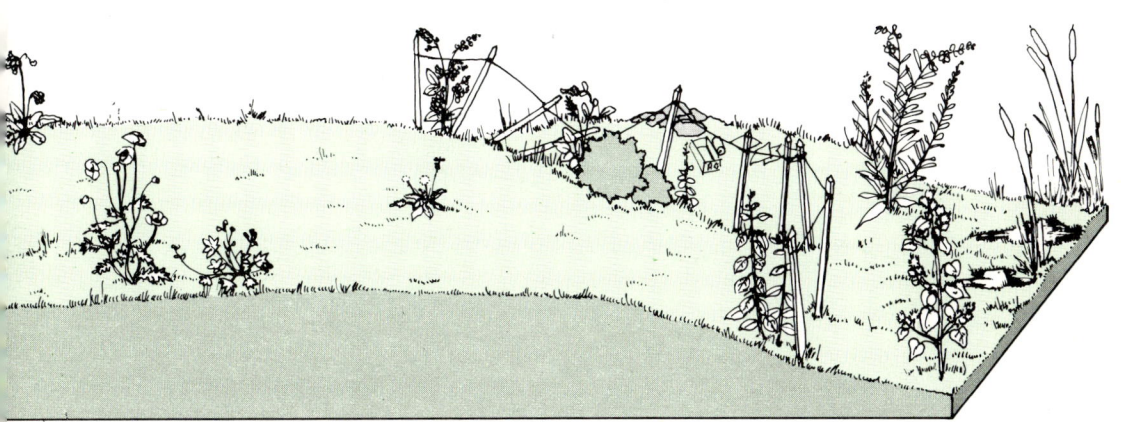

Fields, meadows and wasteland
Betony
Burdock
Chickweed
Cowslip
Dandelion
Foxglove
Henbane
Lady's mantle
Meadowsweet
Mugwort
Nettle
Poppy
Wormwood

Bogs and marsh
Burdock
Meadowsweet
Willow-herb

lady's mantle

LADY'S MANTLE (*Alchemilla vulgaris*). A small, not very conspicuous perennial plant that prefers a coolish climate, lady's mantle is easily recognized by its handsome fan-shaped leaves. These have 7 or 9 lobes at the scalloped edges. It is an all-green plant, including its flowers. These are tiny and appear in loose clusters from June to August. The lower leaves of lady's mantle can be as much as 7 in (18 cm) across and are on long stalks, whereas the upper leaves are almost stalkless.

The herb contains tannin and for this reason has styptic properties that make it useful in cases of bleeding (in herbal medicine it is used to counteract excessive menstruation). It has been regarded as a valuable styptic for centuries and Culpeper wrote, 'Lady's mantle is very proper for inflamed wounds and to stay bleedings, vomitings, fluxes of all sorts, bruises by falls and ruptures. It is one of the most singular wound herbs and therefore highly prized.'

Lady's mantle
Lady's mantle is called Alchemilla because the old alchemists collected dew from its leaves for their healing brews.

burdock

BURDOCK (*Arctium lappa*). A sturdy plant growing between 3 and 4 ft (0.9–1.2 m) high and flourishing in dampish waste places and hedgerows, burdock is noteworthy for the olive green colour of its foliage and for the burrs from which its name is derived. Its heart-shaped lower leaves, which can be 1 ft (30 cm) long, are covered with a fine down on the underside, giving them a greyish appearance. As the leaves ascend the stout stems they become smaller and more oval in shape with less down on the underside. Its florets, or small flowers, in their scaly burrs are sometimes interwoven with a fine cottony down. The burrs catch on anything that is passing, and through their adherence to the coats of passing animals the seeds are carried away to propagate elsewhere.

Burdock has its uses in the kitchen. The stems of the first year's growth can be boiled or steamed in the same way as asparagus: they should be cut before the plant flowers and the skin should be removed. At one time the stems of burdock were candied in much the same way as those of angelica. Its roots are a valuable source of Inulin, a white, starchy substance used in the manufacture of fructose. Burdock is used to treat skin diseases, scurvy and rheumatism.

> **Burdock**
> *Crowned...*
> *With burdocks, hemlock, nettles, cuckoo-flowers, Darnel, and all the idle weeds that grow*
> *In our sustaining corn.*
> Shakespeare (1564–1616)
> *King Lear*

Wormwood

WORMWOOD (*Artemisia absinthium*). This, the common wormwood, is a member of the genus that also includes mugwort. It is a perennial, growing usually on waste or common land, often near the sea. Its strong, branched stems rise to about 2½ ft (75 cm) above the ground, and both stems and leaves are covered with silky hairs, giving them a whitish colour. The leaves are about 3 in (8 cm) long, with pronounced blunted segments. The flowers, yellowish in colour, are like small pendulous spheres hanging in sprays from the flower stems. They bloom from July until autumn. The whole plant is bitter and aromatic.

Wormwood is recognized as a stimulant and a tonic, and is an important ingredient of vermouth and absinthe (note its Latin name). An infusion, wormwood tea, is good for stomach upsets, and the dried and powdered leaves are used as a vermifuge. In olden days the dried leaves were used as an insect repellent. As a 16th-century verse charmingly puts it:
*While Wormwood hath seed
  get a handful or twaine
To save against March,
  to make flea to refraine.*

*O mickle is the powerful
  grace that lies
In herbs, plants, stones,
  and their true qualities.*
Shakespeare (1564–1616)
– *Romeo and Juliet*

mugwort

MUGWORT (*Artemisia vulgaris*). Related to wormwood, this perennial grows in hedges and on wasteland and common land. It grows to a height of 3 ft (90 cm) or so and has no smell. The thin, purplish stems bear smooth, dark green leaves with a thick, white, downy covering on the underside. They are acutely segmented, the segments being sharply pointed. Mugwort flowers from July to September with small reddish or pale yellow blossoms in panicles, or clusters, at the end of the stalks, in much the same sort of formation as oats. The woody roots, which are used in medicine, are about 8 in (20 cm) long, pale brown outside, but white inside with a thick bark. From this main root grow many thinner and shorter rootlets.

The herb is not often used in the kitchen, although it is sometimes an ingredient for stuffing a goose, and in the last century its leaves were sometimes used as a substitute for tea. Before the introduction of hops, the dried flowers of mugwort were used to flavour beer. The leaves and roots are used medicinally today, the leaves making an infusion to be taken at the first sign of a cold and also as a tonic. The roots — lifted in the autumn, washed, and thoroughly dried until they break readily in the hand — are used in cases of nervous disorder and were once regarded as a remedy for epilepsy. In his *Herball*, Gerard declared that it 'cureth the shakings of the joynts inclining to the Palsie.'

Mugwort
*If they would drink nettles in March,
And eat mugwort in May,
So many fine maidens
Wouldn't go to the clay.*
Denham (1846) — *Proverbs*

woodruff

WOODRUFF (*Asperula odorata*). This is an attractive little woodland perennial, anxious to keep in the shade as much as possible. When dried it is sweet-smelling, reminiscent of newly mown hay. It grows up to 1 ft (30 cm) high, with erect smooth stems, and its shiny, bright green leaves grow around the stem in whorls of about 8 leaves like rosettes — a possible explanation for the word *ruff* in its name. These leaves fade in colour if they are exposed to too much sunlight. They are rather rigid in form, with small prickles on their edges. The flowers, which bloom in May and June, are small and white, and the seed, when ripe, is a black-tipped, bristly, little ball, white on the underside. The plant has widely spreading roots.

With its sweet smell of new-mown hay, woodruff was not surprisingly one of the ancient strewing herbs and is still used in pot-pourri and in the linen chest or cupboard. Its fresh young sprigs are used to flavour wine cups and sometimes liqueurs and it is the basis of the German Maibowle (May Cup) drunk to celebrate May Day. Woodruff tea is a refreshing infusion. The herb is used in perfumery and also to disguise the disagreeable smells of medicines to make them easier to take. Its leaves were once believed to be useful for healing wounds.

. . . Herbs and trees bring forth fruit and flourish in May.
Malory (fl. 1470)

deadly nightshade

DEADLY NIGHTSHADE (*Atropa belladonna*). An ominous name for a plant that can be not only ominous but beneficial. It is a bushy perennial growing between 3 and 5 ft (0.9–1.5 m) high, or even higher in favourable conditions under trees or on chalk or limestone. The stem is slightly purple in colour and carries dark green leaves of different sizes, up to 10 in (25 cm) in length. The leaves are pointed at the extremities and have prominent veins on the underside. The flowers, which appear in June and July, grow in the axils of the leaves and are bell-shaped, about 1 in (2 cm) long and dull purple touched with green in colour. The flower is replaced by a smooth black berry about the size of a marble, containing seeds in a sweet, dark juice.

The berry of the deadly nightshade, despite its syrupy taste, is highly poisonous and can cause death, especially to children, which is why it is dangerous to include it in the herb garden. The whole plant is poisonous, but it is cultivated commercially for its medicinal value. It contains two alkaloids, atropine and hyoscyamine. The latter is used as a sedative. Atropine, sometimes called belladonna, is used by ophthalmologists to dilate the pupil of the eye and has the advantage over other drops that the dilation diminishes more rapidly. It is also used by doctors to slow down secretions of sweat and saliva, as an anti-spasmodic and as a liniment.

> Therefore I wol seye a proverb
> That he that fully knoweth t'herbe
> May safely lay it to his eye.
> Chaucer (1340–1400) – The House of Fame

Chapter three

foxglove

FOXGLOVE (*Digitalis purpurea*). This handsome biennial, a familiar sight on the borders of woods, stands up to 6 ft (1.8 m) in height. The tall stems, which eventually bear long spikes of purple, drooping, tubular bell-shaped flowers, do not appear until the second year of growth, the flowers appearing in June or July. The flowers are from 1½ to 2½ in (4–6 cm) long, paler inside than out, and often beautifully spotted inside. The leaves at the base of the stem are large – as much as 1 ft (30 cm) in length – but the leaves diminish in size with the height of the stem. They have very prominent sloping lateral veins, and are rather wrinkled and covered with tiny hairs. After the flowers have fallen from the main stem smaller lateral shoots may grow from the lower part of the plant.

The leaf of the foxglove is poisonous and the herb is, therefore, not used in the kitchen. But the plant is cultivated for important medical uses. The powerful drug digitalis comes from its dried leaves and is used to make the heart beat more regularly and also, when the heart muscles are too weak, to make the blood circulate more normally. It is used also in the treatment of kidney disease.

Foxglove
The foxglove, with its stately bells
Of purple, shall adorn thy dells.
D. M. Moir (1798–1851) – *The Birth of the Flowers*

willow-herb

WILLOW-HERB (*Epilobium angustifolium*). Also known as rosebay, this is the herb that proved its reputation for toughness by springing up on the derelict bomb sites in London during the Second World War. It is not only tough but handsome, and on the whole prefers damp woods to bombed buildings. It grows to a height of from 4 to 8 ft (1.2–2.4 m) and has long, thin, serrated leaves not unlike those of the willow – hence its name. Gerard described it as 'a goodly and stately plant having leaves like the greatest willow or osier, garnished with brave flowers of great beautie, consisting of four leaves apiece of an orient purple colour.' These flowers are about 1 in (2 cm) in diameter and grow in delicate sprays.

In Russia the leaves of the willow-herb are used as a substitute for tea – indeed, they were once used in England for the same purpose. Willow-herb has been used in the treatment of whooping cough and asthma and as an intestinal astringent. In the kitchen the young shoots can be boiled and used in the same way as asparagus.

Willowherb
*And willows,
willow-herb, and grass,
And meadowsweet, and
haycocks dry,
No whit less still and lonely fair
Than the high cloudlets
in the sky.*
Edward Thomas
(1878–1917)

witch hazel

WITCH HAZEL (*Hamamelis virginiana*). This shrub, or rather small tree – it reaches between 10 and 12 feet in height – is a native of the United States and Canada but also grows in Britain. Its branching trunks grow from a single root, have a smooth grey bark and can be as much as 6 in (15 cm) in diameter. They bear alternating leaves, broad and oval, about 4 in (10 cm) long and with spots on the underside. The shrubs bear yellow flowers, which do not appear until after the leaves have fallen in autumn, and these are followed by black nuts. In North America (but not in Britain) these nuts contain white seeds which, when ripe, are vigorously ejected as though shot from a gun – hence the American name snapping hazelnut.

Both leaves and bark (which are used medicinally) contain tannin and can be made into a tea that is useful in checking internal haemorrhage. In fact, the herb is used against all forms of bleeding, and particularly in cases of haemorrhoids. An ointment prepared from it has been a popular form of relief against burns, insect bites, bruises and swellings.

Witch hazel
The twigs of this North American shrub are used for water divining.

henbane

HENBANE (*Hyoscyamus niger*). This is another poisonous wild herb – one that an old writer declared would bring 'frenzie' if eaten. 'Whoso useth more than four leaves,' he declared, 'shall be in danger to sleepe without waking.' Curiously the plant can be either an annual or a biennial. The annual grows to about 2 ft (60 cm) high and flowers in July or August; the biennial is stronger and taller and flowers in May and June of the second year. The biennial produces only a few leaves in the first year, then a rosette of leaves in the second. From this rises a tough, tall stem. The leaves are hairy, long and sharply pointed, with strongly serrated edges, and are a greyish green. The hairs on the leaves cause them to feel sticky. The yellow flowers, sometimes marked with purple, are bell-shaped and have a tough, five-pointed calyx. The plant emits a somewhat disagreeable odour.

Like deadly nightshade, the leaves of henbane contain the alkaloids hyoscyamine and atropine – more of the former than the latter. The drug derived from the herb is used as an antispasmodic and as a sedative to allay hysteria and other nervous ailments. It is milder than similar drugs but is nevertheless a dangerous poison. Used in excess it can cause semi-blindness and even death. Hyoscine, another constituent of henbane, is a strong sedative inducing loss of memory and unconsciousness. Externally henbane can be used as a liniment or poultice.

Henbane
The prospect of finding anybody out in anything would have kept Miss Miggs awake under the influence of henbane.
Dickens (1812–70) – *Barnaby Rudge*

poppy

POPPIES. The two principal varieties of this herb are the red poppy (*Papaver rhoeas*) and the white poppy (*Papaver somniferum*). The latter, as its Latin name suggests, is the poppy from which opium is derived. Both grow wild or can be cultivated. Both are annuals. Both grow about 2 ft (60 cm) high. In Europe the red poppy is the one more commonly seen in the fields. As its name indicates, it has vivid scarlet blooms, but there is a dark spot at the base of each petal. The dark green leaves are deeply indented. The wild white poppy's flower is in fact not white but a very pale mauve, so pale as to be almost white but with a deeper purple stain at the base of the petal.

The seeds of the poppy are harmless and have no narcotic properties. Those of the red poppy are used on the continent of Europe in cakes, and a vegetable oil is also made from them. A syrup useful in allaying coughing is made from the petals. Opium, from which the drug morphine derives, is extracted from the unripe, pale green seed heads of the white poppy.

Poppy
But pleasures are like poppies spread –
You seize the flow'r, its bloom is shed.
Burns (1759–96) – *Tam o'Shanter*

Wild herbs 111

cowslip

COWSLIP (*Primula veris*). As its Latin name indicates, the perennial cowslip is a member of the primrose family. At one time a common sight in meadows and on common land, it is now not so often seen. Its leaves, not unlike those of the primrose but shorter and slightly more heart-shaped, make their appearance in early spring. They form a rosette lying close to the ground and in April or May a single erect stem grows from the centre of this. At its extremity this stem breaks into a number of short stalks, each of which carries a flower, and the effect created is that of a drooping umbel. Each flower grows from a pale green, bell-shaped calyx. The petals are golden yellow, each with a tiny red spot. These flowers measure about ½ in (1 cm) across.

In the 17th century Culpeper wrote of the uses of cowslips in cosmetics. 'Our city dames know well enough,' he wrote, 'how cowslip ointment or distilled water add to beauty or restore it when lost.' Cowslips were also used to cure trembling and palsy – indeed the Greeks called it *Paralysio*. The young leaves were also once used as a salad. In some country places today cowslip wine is still made and much enjoyed. It is in fact a cordial, not a wine. It is made by steeping the petals in sugared spring water with lemon juice and yeast added. The mixture is left to 'work' and then, when it has quietened down, is corked and left to stand for 9 months or so.

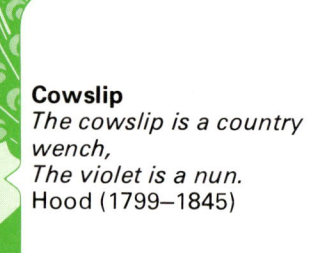

Cowslip
The cowslip is a country wench,
The violet is a nun.
Hood (1799–1845)

Wild herbs

chickweed

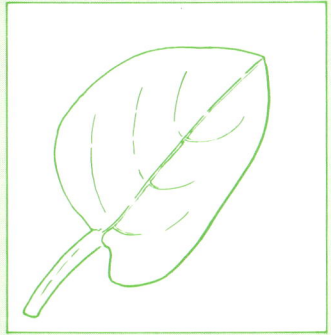

CHICKWEED (*Stellaria media*). Most gardeners are familiar with this annual weed and quickly root it out. Nevertheless it is a plant respected by herbalists for its medicinal qualities and it has some uses in the kitchen. There are many varieties but the most familiar is recognized by its many pale green, succulent branches trailing along the ground and bearing pale green oval leaves about ¼ in (6 mm) wide and twice as long.

Chickweed is unmistakable, for its stems have a remarkable peculiarity. A thin line of hairs runs up the stem on one side until it reaches a pair of leaves, when it switches to the other side; it continues alternating after each pair of leaves. At night the leaves move together to form a protective covering for the new shoots. The small, white, star-shaped flowers continue from March to autumn.

The young leaves of chickweed can be eaten raw in green salads and can be used cooked in much the same way as spinach. The leaves, chopped and boiled in lard, are recognized by herbalists as a good ointment for sores and skin diseases. In this connection three centuries ago Culpeper was fulsome in his praise. 'The leaves of Chickweed,' he said, 'boyled in water very soft, adding thereto some hog's grease, the powder of Fennugreeke and Linseed, and a few roots of Marsh Mallows, and stamped to the form of a cataplasme or pultesse, taketh away the swelling of the legs or any other part . . . it comforteth, digesteth, defendeth, and suppurateth very notably.'

meadow-sweet

MEADOWSWEET (*Spiraea ulmaria*). Also known as queen of the meadows, this handsome plant of fields and banks well deserves its title. It blooms from June to the end of August, stands from 2 to 4 ft (60–120 cm) high and is noteworthy for its fragrance. The herbalist Gerard wrote that the leaves and flowers of meadowsweet 'farre excelle all other strewing herbs for to deck up houses . . . for the smell thereof makes the heart merrie and joyful and delighteth the senses.' The whole plant is scented but the perfume of the leaves is different from that of the flowers. Its leaves are serrated, the large terminal leaflets, up to 3 in (8 cm) long, having 3 lobes. They are dark green on the upper side, downy beneath. The flowers, which appear in June, are small and yellowish white and grow in clusters.

In mediaeval times the flowers of the meadowsweet were used to flavour wines and beers, and the whole plant, as Gerard says, was used as a strewing herb. The plant contains such minerals as iron, phosphorus, sodium and sulphur, and in herbal medicine is used in cases of diarrhoea and stomach upsets.

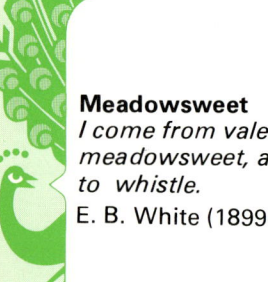

Meadowsweet
I come from vales of meadowsweet, and I love to whistle.
E. B. White (1899–   )

Betony
. . . a sentry of dark betonies,
The stateliest of small flowers on earth,
At the forest verge.
Edward Thomas (1878–1917)

betony

BETONY (*Stachys betonica*). A perennial, also known as bishopswort, this plant is usually found in woods and hedges, but also grows in open spaces. It is a pretty plant growing to between 1 and 2 ft (30–60 cm) high, with two forms of leaves — those that grow on stalks from the root and are heart-shaped, and those that grow, stalkless, from the stems. These leaves are from 2 to 3 in (4–6 cm) long and rather widely separated. The plant's thin stems are square and grooved and the whole plant is slightly hairy. Betony blooms in July and August, the rich, red-purple flowers growing in a spike at the extremities of the stems with a length of bare stem below, then more flowers — a peculiarity of the plant. If the flowers are fertilized, small brown, smooth and triangular nuts appear.

To old herbalists betony was a herb with many virtues ranging from warding off evil spirits to curing the bite of a mad dog. It had (and still has) a reputation for relieving headaches when made into an infusion of 1 oz (28 gm) of the dried herb to 1 pt (0.5 l) of boiling water. The leaves should be gathered in July and dried. The herb is used in conjunction with other medicines in the treatment of head pains, neuralgia and nervous troubles. It was once used in snuff as a cure for headaches, and as far back as the 17th century it was mentioned as a cure for 'the most obstinate headaches' by 'daily breakfasting *for a month or six weeks* on a decoction of betony made with new milk and strained.'

dandelion

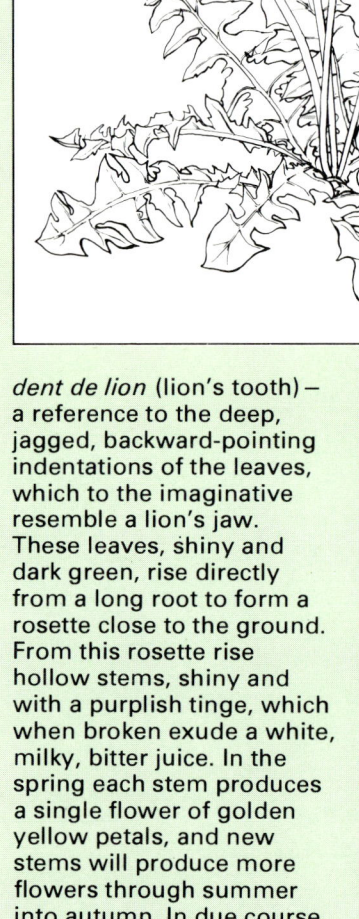

DANDELION (*Taraxacum officinale*). Although generally thought of as a tiresome weed the ubiquitous dandelion is widely used in the kitchen and has valuable medicinal properties. It is popularly believed that its name derives from the French *dent de lion* (lion's tooth) — a reference to the deep, jagged, backward-pointing indentations of the leaves, which to the imaginative resemble a lion's jaw. These leaves, shiny and dark green, rise directly from a long root to form a rosette close to the ground. From this rosette rise hollow stems, shiny and with a purplish tinge, which when broken exude a white, milky, bitter juice. In the spring each stem produces a single flower of golden yellow petals, and new stems will produce more flowers through summer into autumn. In due course the flowers are replaced by the familiar gossamer seed heads, which drift in the wind to ensure further propagation.

The resentment that gardeners tend to have against the dandelion is by no means shared by everyone. Statistically it contains 12 times the Vitamin A of a lettuce and about three times its Vitamin C. Its young leaves — the bigger leaves are bitter — can be used in salads and may be cooked, like spinach, as a green vegetable. Its flowers are used to make dandelion wine — one of the more comforting of the cottage wines. Even the roots have a culinary use, for they can be roasted and ground as an artificial 'coffee.' The juice from the roots is used in medicine, especially in kidney and liver disorders and as a tonic in cases of dyspepsia.

> **Dandelion**
> With locks of gold today;
> Tomorrow silver grey;
> Then blossom-bald.
> Behold,
> O man, thy fortune told!
> J. B. Tabb (1845–1909)

nettle

Nettle
Nettle's tender shoots, to cleanse the blood.
Gay (1685–1732)

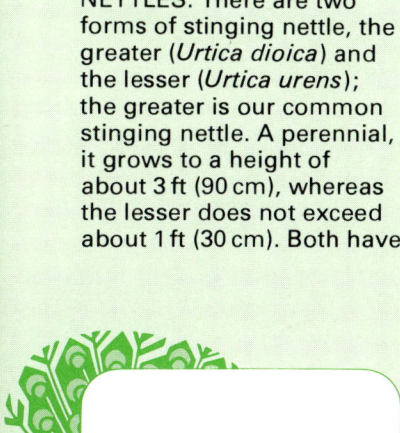

NETTLES. There are two forms of stinging nettle, the greater (*Urtica dioica*) and the lesser (*Urtica urens*); the greater is our common stinging nettle. A perennial, it grows to a height of about 3 ft (90 cm), whereas the lesser does not exceed about 1 ft (30 cm). Both have fine hairs on leaves and stems; when these pierce the human skin, they inject a poison that immediately causes irritation and some inflammation. The nettle has thin yellow roots that spread widely just below the surface of the soil and bring about rapid expansion of the nettle crops when once established. It is said that if nettles are cut down three times in three consecutive years they will be eradicated. The leaves of the greater variety are heart-shaped, coming to a point, whereas those of the lesser are smaller and rounder, but both are finely toothed. The flowers of both are green and appear in July and August in pendulous clusters.

The despised nettle has many surprising uses. There was a time when its fibres rivalled those of flax for making linen, and they were used to make twine for fishing nets. In his diary Samuel Pepys writes of nettle pudding, 'which was very good.' Today many people use nettles as a vegetable, cooking the young leaves gathered in spring and summer like spinach. Country folk use the young tops of the plant to make a refreshing type of beer. Nettles have for long had a reputation for arresting bleeding and in the treatment of rheumatism. In homeopathic medicine they are used against asthma, and they are also the basis for a hair lotion.

chapter four
how to use herbs

119

Pictures from Mrs Beeton's famous cookery book, 1901.

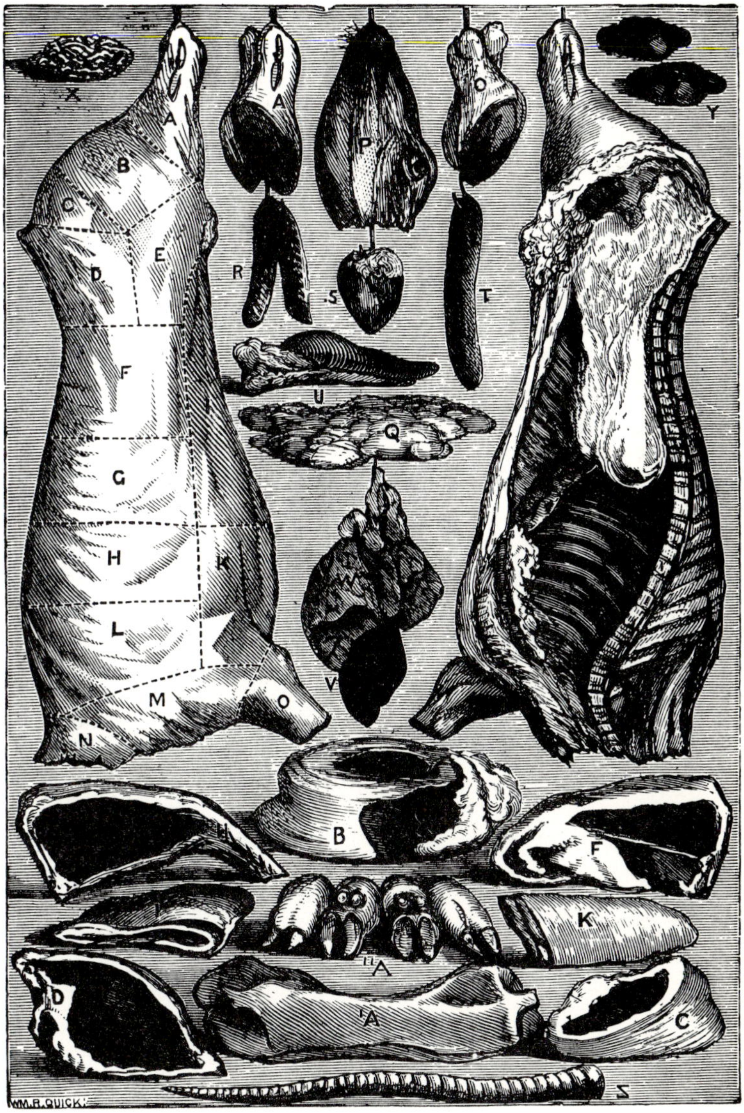

Broadly speaking, herbs can be used in three main ways: in cooking for the purpose of adding flavour; for their qualities of fragrance, in the manufacture of toilet preparations and cosmetics; and in medicine. Some herbs, indeed, are included in all these categories.

The use of herbs in cooking is very much a matter of personal taste, and anyone can become an expert in the use of culinary herbs in the kitchen, with practice. It is much the same with the sweet herbs, which our forebears often called 'strewing herbs', which are used for their fragrance, although of course the manufacture of the more exotic perfumes calls for special knowledge and training. As for the medicinal use of herbs, it is perhaps best to leave this to the experts, although you don't need to be an expert to make the simple tisanes or herb teas.

Originally there were two basic reasons for using herbs and spices in food. One, of course, was to add interesting new flavours, but perhaps more important was their use to overpower the disagreeable flavour of poorly preserved meat, fish and game. We can scarcely imagine what life was like when there were no refrigerators or tin cans, and meat had to be preserved for the winter by pickling or salting. Meals must have been very boring, and sometimes unpleasant, and it is not surprising that our forefathers – or more likely our foremothers – should have added the scented leaves that they had noticed on the plants growing nearby and probably tasted out of curiosity. As for the sweet herbs, their use is also understandable. Baths, like drainage, were uncommon, and evil smells from both persons and places must have been everywhere. So herbs were strewn on the floor and this was not only because they smelled pleasant when walked on, but also because some of them were believed to be an insect repellent. Personal hygiene was poor indeed, and any eminent personage walking in a crowded area might carry a pomander or a nosegay of fresh herbs to discourage fleas and to counteract the unpleasant smells around him on all sides.

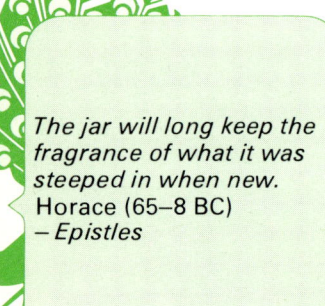

The jar will long keep the fragrance of what it was steeped in when new.
Horace (65–8 BC)
– *Epistles*

Incense was probably first burned in temples and churches for the same reason. Pomanders, pot-pourri, sachets, and toilet waters were introduced not just because they were pleasant to have around the house, but because they were useful too.

It is not without significance that the authors of two of the most famous English Herbals, Gerard and Culpeper, were connected with medicine, Gerard being a barber surgeon and Culpeper a physician. But long before they wrote, the connection between herbs and health had been firmly established. Socrates knew about hemlock, and Pliny wrote about the virtues of betony. In mediaeval times the local witch and the more respectable apothecary shared a risky, but often very hypothetical, knowledge of the medicinal qualities of herbs. These they used to cure a wide range of sicknesses, ranging from unrequited love to rheumatism, palsy and the healing of wounds. Medical treatment in those days must have been one of life's greatest hazards.

But we should not mock them too much, and talk of old wives' tales. Modern medicine, taking a variety of forms such as pills, ointments and injections, is very much based on the chemical contents of herbs, and it is astonishing how many of them are used in the treatment of those ills with which they were associated by the witches and apothecaries of centuries ago.

This last chapter concentrates very much on the practical uses to which herbs can be put. In short it explains why they are really worth growing, particularly as most of them make very little demand on the soil, and not much demand on the gardener. Besides the pleasure that growing herbs give in the garden or window-box, they lend themselves to endless experiments in cookery. In this chapter there are hints on how to dry and store herbs for the kitchen, and how to use them; there are a number of basic recipes, including several wines and teas. Then there are suggestions for other ways of using herbs around the home and for delightful gifts.

> *But from the mountain's grassy side*
> *A guiltless feast I bring;*
> *A scrip with herbs and fruits supplied*
> *And water from the spring.*
> Goldsmith (1728–74)

drying herbs

Drying herbs is not a difficult process, but it does call for some care and thought. The leaves of most herbs preserve their flavour and (just as important) their colour only if they are gathered at the right time and dried away from direct sunlight. The fresh green herb at the right season undoubtedly imparts the finer flavour, but the dried herb is much stronger, and only a pinch is needed where you might have to use a handful or more of fresh leaves.

Generally the best time to gather herbs is just before the plant blooms, when it has its strongest flavour and contains the maximum of essential oils. But rosemary and thyme are both gathered when the plants are in full flower. Leaves need to be dried quickly unless they are very thick, but seeds are dried slowly. Some herbs are best preserved hanging in bunches, but the most practical way is to crumble the dried leaves in one's hands, and to store them in airtight jars in a cupboard. Jars should be labelled with the herb's name and the date.

Mint and Fennel
*Then went I forth on my right hand,
Downe by a litel path I found
Of Mintes full and Fennell greene.*
Chaucer (1340–1400) — *Roman de la Rose*

Balm	Does not dry well.
Basil	Cut sprigs on a dry day just before flowering. Handle as little as possible. Hang sprigs in bunches in a warm airy cupboard, or dry in a slow oven at 100°F. Strip leaves from stems when dry, crumble them gently by hand, and store in airtight containers.
Bay	Dry leaves in layers on trays, in a warm (but not hot) shady place. Press the dried leaves under books or boards to prevent curling, before storing whole in jars.
Borage	Does not dry well.
Camomile	Pick the flowers when they are completely dry and fully open. Dry them quickly in a single layer on a ventilated tray. Store in airtight containers.
Chervil	Does not dry well.
Chives	Do not dry well.
Dill	For other uses than pickling, seeds should be gathered when brown. Pick the whole seed heads, and shake off the seeds over paper. For pickling, cut when the flowers are still on the stalks: spread out the seeds and dry without any artificial heat.
Elder	Gather berries when they are black, in autumn, and dry on trays until they are slightly wrinkled.
Fennel	Leaves do not dry well. Pick seed heads when brown, and hang them in a paper bag till completely dry.

How to use herbs 123

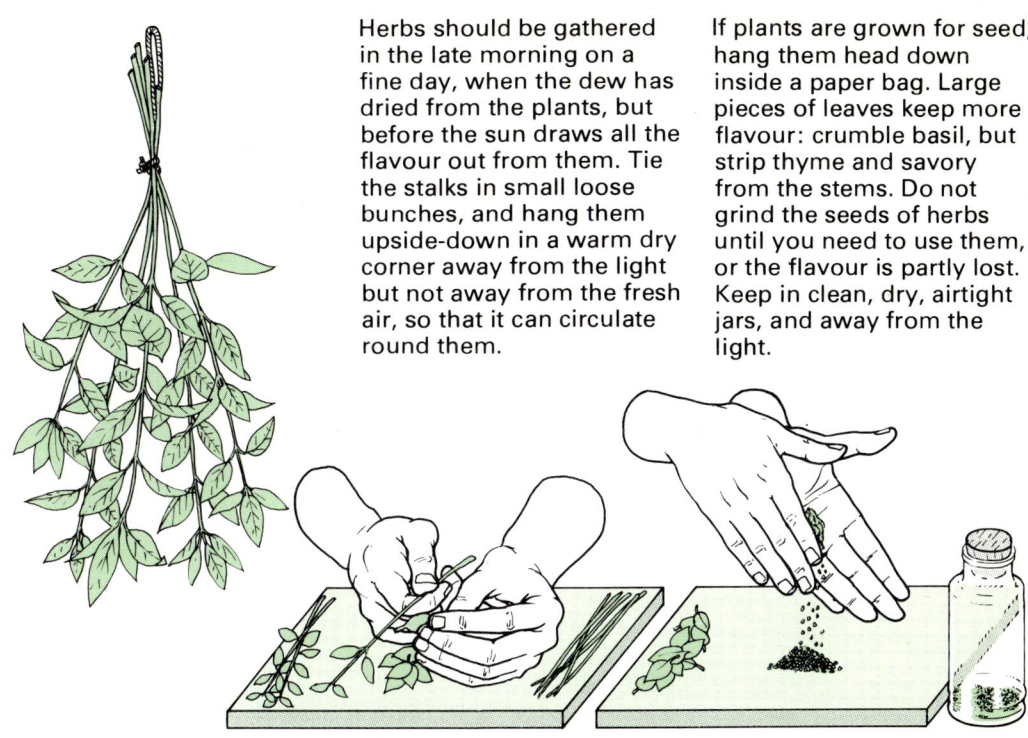

Herbs should be gathered in the late morning on a fine day, when the dew has dried from the plants, but before the sun draws all the flavour out from them. Tie the stalks in small loose bunches, and hang them upside-down in a warm dry corner away from the light but not away from the fresh air, so that it can circulate round them.

If plants are grown for seed, hang them head down inside a paper bag. Large pieces of leaves keep more flavour: crumble basil, but strip thyme and savory from the stems. Do not grind the seeds of herbs until you need to use them, or the flavour is partly lost. Keep in clean, dry, airtight jars, and away from the light.

Lady's mantle	Gather leaves while the plants are in flower. Dry them in the dark, in a well-ventilated place that is not too hot.
Lovage	The leaves, when light green, can be dried in a cool oven and then stored in airtight containers.
Marjoram	Gather in the morning when the plant is about to flower. Dry in layers in a dark, warm place; the temperature should not exceed 100°F.
Mint	Sprigs may be hung in bunches in the dark, allowing free circulation of air. When dry, strip the leaves from the stalks and rub them. Store in glass jars in the dark.
Parsley	Before drying young summer and autumn parsley sprigs, wash them well. Lay on trays and dry in the dark as quickly as possible in a low oven (100°F), leaving the door slightly open.
Rosemary	Gather the sprigs in early autumn, and dry them in the dark on trays in a well-ventilated cupboard.
Sage	Sprigs cut just before flowering can be hung in bunches permitting the free circulation of air. Drying takes longer than with most other herbs.
Tarragon	Cut the sprigs as flowering begins. Hang them in bunches in the dark at a moderate temperature. Strip and crumble the leaves when completely dry, and store them in airtight containers.
Thyme	As for tarragon.

Chapter four

herbs in the kitchen

The normally equipped kitchen is quite capable of dealing with all the problems arising from the use of herbs, but there are some special tools that can make life much easier for the cook. To begin with, if you are growing your own herbs you will need something bigger than the small decorative glass jars in which herbs are usually sold in the shops. Instant coffee jars are excellent for the purpose, either the 4 oz (112 gm) size or the 8 oz (224 gm) one, but you will probably find other empty jars that are

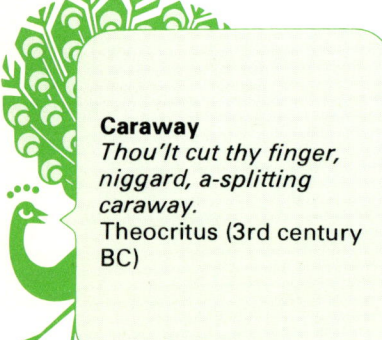

Caraway
Thou'lt cut thy finger, niggard, a-splitting caraway.
Theocritus (3rd century BC)

One of the traditional tools used by the herbalist is the pestle and mortar, with which he crushed the seeds and leaves to extract their oils and flavour, and then blended the different herbs together. A pestle and mortar can be made of wood, stone or ceramics. They are a most useful tool to buy if you intend to use herbs often.

It is rather hard work to chop herbs in any quantity with a plain knife, and a proper chopping blade can make the job much easier. By holding the two handles, one in each hand, and making a seesawing motion of the blade, you can quickly chop herbs on a chopping board. The tool can also be used for preparing vegetables.

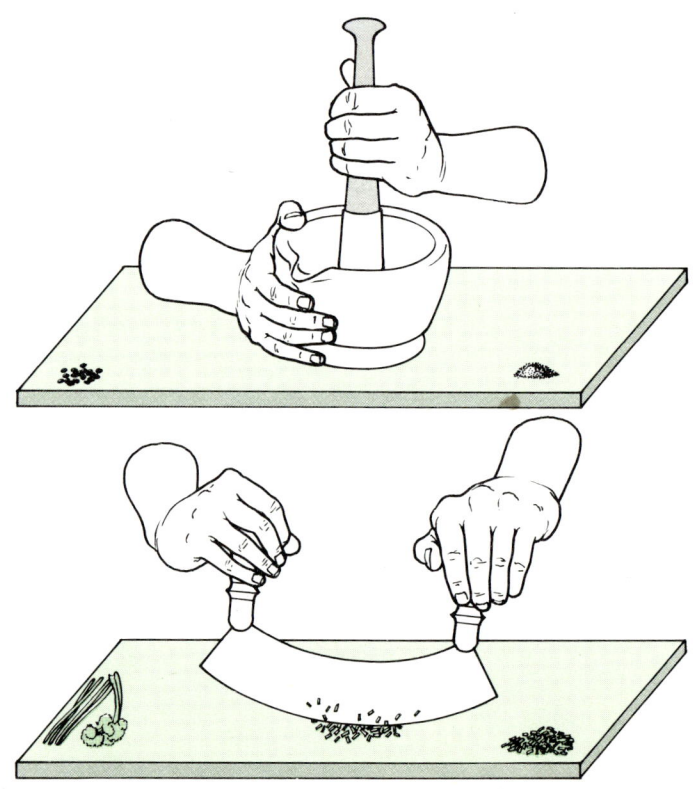

equally convenient; they must have a good screw-on lid to keep the herbs airtight. You can buy labels printed with the names of herbs and spices, and these can make your collection look nostalgically like an old herbalist's shop. In any case, do label all the herbs as you put them into jars, because many of them look very similar once they have been dried. The jars should all be kept inside a cupboard, not on an open shelf, where the light and warmth will rapidly make them lose their flavour and colour.

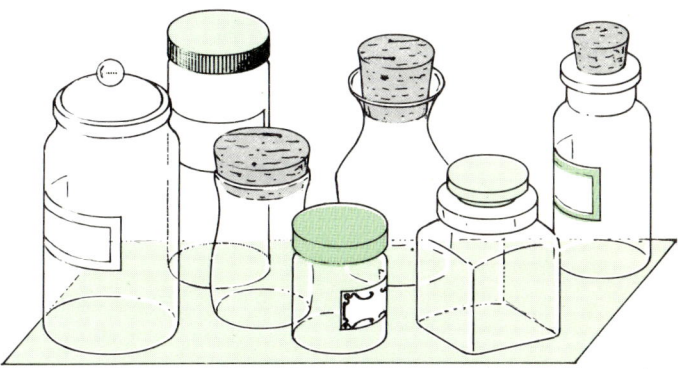

The parsley mill shown here is a very useful French tool for the kitchen; it can be used for chopping not only parsley, but many other herbs too.

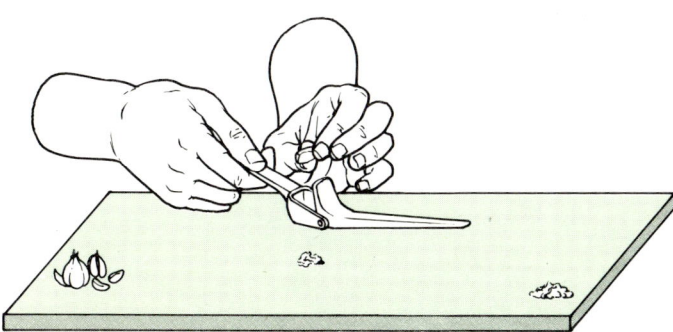

If you are an enthusiast for garlic, you will find a garlic crusher a most useful gadget to have in the kitchen, and avoid having your fingers always scented with garlic. It is advisable to skin the clove of garlic first, before putting it into the crusher.

SALADS	SAUCES	SOUPS	STEWS
Anise leaves ⓢ		**Anise** leaves and seeds	**Anise** leaves and seeds
Balm leaves	**Balm** leaves		
	Basil leaves	**Basil** leaves	
			Bay leaves ⓢ
Borage leaves and flowers		**Borage** leaves and flowers	
Caraway leaves		**Caraway** leaves	**Caraway** seeds
Chervil leaves		**Chervil** leaves	
Chives chopped	**Chives** chopped	**Chives**	**Chives**
Dill leaves			
Fennel leaves chopped		**Fennel** leaves chopped	
Garlic ⓢ	**Garlic**	**Garlic** ⓢ	**Garlic** ⓢ
	Horseradish grated root		
Hyssop flowers and young shoots chopped ⓢ		**Hyssop** flowers and young shoots chopped ⓢ	
			Juniper berries
Lovage leaves and young shoots		**Lovage** leaves and young shoots	
Marjoram	**Marjoram**		
	Mint leaves chopped		
Nasturtium leaves			
Parsley chopped	**Parsley** chopped	**Parsley**	
Purslane leaves			
		Rosemary ⓢ	**Rosemary**
		Saffron	
		Sage leaves	**Sage** leaves
Salad burnet	**Salad burnet**	**Salad burnet**	
Savory		**Savory**	
Sorrel		**Sorrel**	
Sweet cicely		**Sweet cicely**	
Tarragon	**Tarragon**		**Tarragon**
Thyme ⓢ		**Thyme**	

ⓢ sparingly

ⓖ generously

Sage
It quickeneth the senses and memory, strengtheneth the sinews, restoreth health to those that have the palsy, and taketh away shakey trembling of the members.
Gerard (1545–1612)

How to use herbs

A bouquet garni
Many recipes, especially soups and casseroles, call for the inclusion of a *bouquet garni* to impart a delicate herb flavour. The composition of a *bouquet garni* varies considerably. Traditionally it is said to consist of small sprigs of thyme, parsley and marjoram and a bay leaf, tied up in a bunch with a strong thread and immersed in the pot during the cooking period (but removed before serving). Another pleasant bunch of herbs consists of a sprig each of thyme, sage, parsley and marjoram, made up in a similar way. Yet another variation is made up of one sprig each of basil, marjoram and thyme, with two sprigs of parsley. Any available herb can be included; try celery, dill, rosemary or tarragon, as well as those already mentioned. It is convenient to use a good length of thread when tying the *bouquet garni* together, so that the end of the thread can be left hanging out of the pot; often it is tied around the saucepan handle. This extra string means that the herbs can be easily taken out of the pot after the cooking is done, thus avoiding having to search around for it with a spoon. If you make up the *bouquet garni* in similar proportions but made of freshly dried herbs in a small muslin bag, tied with a strong thread, it is very convenient to store and to use; several of these in an attractive box make a most useful gift.

Herb vinegars
Plain white wine vinegar or cider vinegar can be pleasantly flavoured with any one of several herbs, including basil, chervil, dill, marjoram, tarragon and thyme. Herb vinegars are pleasant in mayonnaise. Place several bruised sprays of fresh herbs into a full bottle of vinegar, put the lid on, and leave in a sunny place (such as a windowsill) for about 2 weeks, before removing the herbs and straining the vinegar. Blends of several different herbs can be used in the same way: one popular recipe uses equal quantities of basil, borage, chives and mint.

Sauce fines herbes to serve with fish
First you need to make a velouté sauce. For this, make a roux with flour and melted butter. Add 1 pt (0.5 l) of boiling fish stock flavoured with salt, peppercorns and lemon juice. Blend well over a low heat, then simmer gently until reduced by one third. Strain into a bowl. Now that the sauce is made, you should have ready 1 tablespoonful each of chopped parsley, chopped chives, chopped shallots and butter, 1 teaspoonful each of fresh tarragon and chervil, and ¼ pt (142 ml) of double cream. Cook the shallots in the butter till soft. Add them and the cream to 1 pt (0.5 l) of velouté sauce. Bring to boil, sieve, and add herbs.

Herb butters
Cream and beat ½ lb (227 gm) of butter, preferably unsalted, in a bowl. Then add 1 oz (28 gm) of chopped and pounded herbs such as chervil, lovage, mint, parsley or tarragon, or a blend of several. Mix until the herbs are completely blended with the creamed butter. To make garlic butter, add to the same amount of butter 1 oz (28 gm) of parsley and 1½ oz (42 gm) of garlic that have first been pounded together with a pestle and mortar. These herb butters are excellent with potatoes or on hot new bread; and garlic is the classic accompaniment for snails. Herb butters can be pressed into small fancy jars and make an unusual gift.

128 Chapter four

MEAT	FISH	POULTRY, GAME	EGG and CHEESE
Balm chopped leaves	**Balm** chopped leaves	**Balm** chopped leaves	
Basil chopped leaves with other herbs Ⓢ	**Basil** chopped leaves Ⓢ	**Basil** chopped leaves Ⓢ	**Basil** chopped leaves Ⓢ
Bay single leaf Ⓢ	**Bay** single leaf Ⓢ		
Caraway seeds with veal or pork		**Caraway** seeds with goose	
Chervil as a mild alternative to parsley Ⓖ	**Chervil** chopped leaves Ⓖ	**Chervil** chopped leaves Ⓖ	**Chervil** chopped leaves with egg dishes Ⓖ
Dill leaves and seeds	**Dill** seeds	**Dill** leaves and seeds	**Dill** seeds
Fennel good with fatty meats Ⓢ	**Fennel** Ⓢ		**Fennel** Ⓢ
Finocchio as fennel above	**Finocchio**		
Garlic Ⓢ			**Garlic** Ⓢ
Horseradish grated root with beef	**Horseradish** grated root with smoked fish		
Hyssop chopped leaves with fatty meat		**Hyssop** chopped leaves with fatty game	
Lovage leaves and seeds		**Lovage** leaves and seeds	
Marjoram chopped leaves		**Marjoram** chopped leaves	**Marjoram** chopped leaves
Mint chopped leaves in sugared vinegar with roast lamb			
			Nasturtium leaves with cream cheese
Parsley chopped leaves in white sauce with boiled gammon and as garnish	**Parsley** in white sauce with steamed or boiled fish and as garnish Ⓢ		**Parsley** chopped for flavour or garnish
Rosemary chopped leaves Ⓢ	**Rosemary** chopped leaves Ⓢ	**Rosemary** chopped leaves Ⓢ	**Rosemary** with some egg dishes Ⓢ
Sage chopped leaves and onion with pork Ⓢ		**Sage** chopped leaves and onion with duck Ⓢ	**Sage** chopped leaves in cheese Ⓢ
Tarragon chopped leaves	**Tarragon** chopped leaves	**Tarragon** chopped leaves	
Thyme chopped leaves in sausages, or with lamb, pork or steak Ⓢ			**Thyme** with cream cheese Ⓢ

How to use herbs

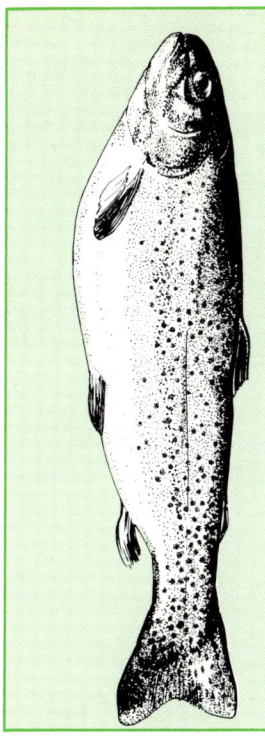

Court-bouillon for fish
A great many poached and boiled fish dishes in French cookery have as their basis a *court-bouillon*, and herbs are an important ingredient of this. A *court-bouillon* is simply a stock that is cooked quickly. The stock ingredients are any fish trimmings, chopped celery, onion, carrots, chopped parsley, thyme, a bay leaf, cloves, water and a little cooking oil. The whole is simmered for about half an hour, peppercorns being added in the last 10 minutes only, and the liquid is strained off for use.

Roast chicken with a difference
This is a dish that gives fragrance to the kitchen while cooking, and it has a delicious flavour when eaten. Prepare a chicken for roasting in the usual way, but with a sharp knife make a short slit in the skin of the breast on either side. Into this, stuff a little dried tarragon and a little butter. Also take 1 oz (28 gm) or more of butter, and mix in salt, pepper, a little garlic and 1 tablespoonful of tarragon. Put this mixture inside the chicken, and then roast it in the usual way.

Stuffing for poultry
Mix together 1 cupful of breadcrumbs with 2 teaspoonfuls of any mixture of dried sage, thyme, marjoram or parsley. Add 1 tablespoonful of chopped onion, ½ oz (14 gm) of soft butter and some seasoning. Mix all these with the yolk of an egg, or a little milk.

Sage and onion stuffing
Peel 4 big onions and boil for 5 minutes. Put 10 leaves of fresh sage into the water to boil for 1 minute only. Chop the sage and onions and mix them thoroughly with 1 oz (28 gm) melted butter, 4 oz (112 gm) breadcrumbs and seasoning. This stuffing is used with roast goose and pork.

Fennel sauce
Make a sauce with 1½ oz (42 gm) flour, 1½ oz (42 gm) margarine and 1 pt (6 dl) stock, with the roux method. Add 4 tablespoonfuls of chopped fennel, 4 teaspoonfuls of sugar, 1½ tablespoonfuls of vinegar and the yolk of an egg, and heat for 1 minute, then add seasoning to taste. Serve with fish or boiled mutton.

Mint sauce
Chop finely a few sprigs of fresh mint, and mix it with vinegar and one teaspoonful of sugar. Prepare this about 2 hours before it is needed, to allow the flavours to blend completely. Serve with roast lamb.

Parsley sauce
Make a white sauce with 1 oz (28 gm) flour, 1 oz (28 gm) margarine and 1 pt (6 dl) milk, by the roux method. Add 4 tablespoonfuls of chopped fresh parsley, and seasoning. If serving this sauce with fish, add 1 tablespoonful of lemon juice or vinegar at the last moment. It can also be served with eggs.

Horseradish sauce
Stir together 2 tablespoonfuls of grated horseradish and ¼ pt (1.5 dl) of *either* white sauce *or* whipped cream, with 2 teaspoonfuls of lemon juice, 1 teaspoonful of sugar and a pinch of salt. This sauce is usually served with beef.

the most useful herbs

This advice is for the modest newcomer to the herb game, who perhaps has no garden. Mint and parsley are probably the herbs most used, especially in late spring and summer. You may be lucky enough to have a herb bed just outside the kitchen door; if it is at the other end of the garden, keep a bunch of fresh mint and parsley in the kitchen, in a tumbler of water – it looks and smells good as well as being convenient. Even the flat-dweller may be able to grow them in window-boxes (see page 14) or in pots indoors. If home growing is impossible, then buy them fresh at the greengrocer's or dried out of season. Don't be misled by the huge stands containing scores of different herbs and spices in fancy jars, which you see in the supermarkets and gift shops; even the great hotel kitchens don't need such a vast supply. In fact, if you are planning to make a dish requiring special herbs, it is better to buy a small quantity for that occasion rather than having a large quantity steadily losing all its flavour while it clutters up

Below is a rough guide to the use of some of the more common culinary herbs. But use it only as a guide: in herbs, as in most things, tastes differ. Some people enjoy lots of garlic, but others dislike it altogether. If entertaining, take your guests' tastes into account or use herbs sparingly.

Basil	Cooking increases the flavour of this herb, so use it with some caution.
Bay leaf	One moderate-size leaf is usually sufficient. It is as well to taste your dish when partly cooked, and be ready to remove the bay leaf if the dish is over-flavoured.
Chervil	Use this generously but do not add it to the dish until the very last moment, because cooking tends to destroy its delicate flavour.
Chives	Use sparingly throughout the cooking period.
Cumin	Use sparingly; a good pinch of the seed is usually enough.
Dill	Use the strongly flavoured seeds sparingly. They are sometimes ground before use.
Fennel	Fish may be baked or grilled on a bed of fennel, or a sprig of the herb can be inserted in the fish. Seeds are also used sparingly in meat stews and fish dishes. Use throughout the cooking period.
Garlic	Very strong flavour – a little goes a very long way.
Hyssop	Rub game with half a teaspoonful of the chopped herb before putting into the oven.

the kitchen shelves. It is better to err on the side of caution while experimenting on the correct quantity to use; some herbs are far stronger in flavour than others, and must be used not only sparingly but also at the right moment in the cooking process. Remember that too generous a use of strong herbs will not only over-flavour the dish you are cooking, but may also cancel out the milder taste of more delicate herbs. Do as the best cooks do, and taste as you go, adding a little more of this and that as required.

You will certainly find it unnecessary to stock more than half a dozen herbs or so at first. Get to know them thoroughly. Herbs that are constantly in use — and all of them herbs that keep well — are basil, bay leaves, marjoram, rosemary, sage, tarragon and thyme. When you can use these well, introduce others gradually.

Juniper	Use about half a dozen berries to flavour stewed game or the gravy for roasts.
Lovage	Leaves can be cooked in stews for the whole cooking period. If using the seeds, remove them before serving.
Marjoram	Use carefully, as this is stronger than most herbs. Rub on joints before roasting.
Mint	Use generously or sparingly according to taste.
Parsley	Use generously with many dishes. Add some more at the end of cooking to bring out additional flavour. Can also be used as a garnish.
Rosemary	Use with caution: its flavour, though delicious and aromatic, is powerful.
Sage	Another strongly-flavoured herb, requiring sparing use.
Tarragon	Can be used generously throughout the full cooking period.
Thyme	Use in moderation, because strongly flavoured. It can be lightly rubbed on joints or fish before cooking.

home-made wines

Few of us, sipping liqueurs and other comforting drinks, could analyze their contents and identify the herbs that contribute to their distinctive flavours. Indeed, many of them are trade secrets. Some flavours are not too difficult to detect, such as the mint flavour of Crême de Menthe, anise in Anisette and caraway in Kummel. It is widely known that juniper berries are used in gin. Perhaps it is more surprising to discover that among the flavourings contained in Chartreuse, for example, are hyssop, spearmint, lemon balm and sweet cicely. Spearmint is used in Bénédictine, wormwood in Vermouth, camomile in one type of sherry (Manzanilla) and many herbs in other drinks. But there are also the cottage 'wines' made from herbs, and very potent some of them are, too. Of course, they are not really wines in the strict sense, because they do not come from the fermented fruit of the vine, but the effect can be very similar even if the taste is not the same. Here are two country beverages based on herbs.

Mint
When the Mint is in the liquor and its fragrance on the glass.
Clarence Ousley (1863–1948) — When the Mint is in the Liquor

For making wine, you will need several items of equipment, all of which must be spotlessly clean, or the wine will be spoilt. You need a plastic bucket in which to mix the various ingredients; a saucepan for cooking the ingredients or heating water; Campden tablets for sterilizing; and some yeast (preferably not brewer's yeast).

You also need a long-handled wooden spoon for mixing the ingredients, and a cover (preferably made of plastic or of a fine-weave fabric) to keep insects and germs out of the bucket.

The wine will need to be sieved through a nylon (not metal) sieve, and a funnel will also be needed to pour the wine into the demi-john, and later into bottles.

How to use herbs 133

Dandelion wine
Over every gallon (4.5 litres) of flowers pour 1 gall (4.5 l) of boiling water. Stir well, cover, and stir occasionally, for 3 days. Strain off the liquid, and add 3 lb (1.4 kg) sugar for every gallon of flowers, a little orange and lemon peel and some bruised root ginger. Boil for 30 minutes and when the liquid is cold put in a little yeast on a piece of toast. Cover for 2 days to allow the yeast to work, bottle the wine, and keep it for several months.

Elderberry wine
Put 1½ gall (6.8 l) of elderberries into a pan and pour over them 1 gall (4.5 l) of boiling water. Keep covered in a warm place for 24 hours, then press out the juice and strain into another pan. For each gallon of the liquid, add ½ oz (14 gm) ginger, ¼ oz (7 gm) cloves and 3 lb (1.4 kg) sugar. Boil slowly for 20 minutes and when almost cool strain into a stone jar, adding a little yeast on toast. When the wine has ceased working, seal the jar and keep for 6 months.

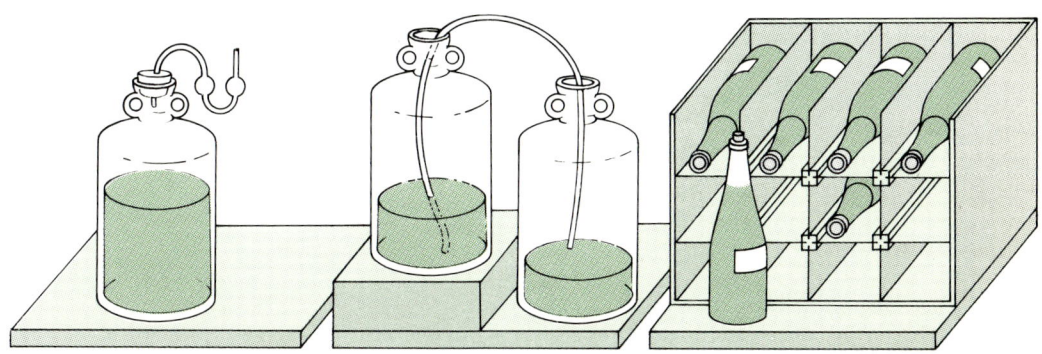

An air lock or fermentation lock allows the gases that are produced during the fermenting process to escape, but prevents the germs and dust particles in the air from entering the demi-john and spoiling the wine.

A siphon is just a length of plastic or rubber tubing with which wine is moved from one container to another in such a way that the sediment is left behind in the old container. The wine should be allowed to stand for some hours before siphoning, to give the sediment time in which to settle.

When the wine has been poured into bottles and firmly corked, the bottles must be stored for some time: white wines are better stored for at least three months after making, and red ones for up to a year. A special wine rack is a great asset, because the wine bottles must be stored lying on their sides, so that the corks remain wet.

herb teas

In the early days before tea was imported from China and India, herb teas were much in use by rich and poor alike. When tea was first imported, it was very expensive, and herb teas were still used by the poor. Then they largely fell into disuse, and have only recently been rediscovered and enjoyed by many. Herb teas are one of the easiest ways in which to make use of home-grown leaves and seeds from the garden, and one of the best ways to taste the full flavour of the plant. Many herb teas are said to have medicinal properties too, which is an added bonus.

Herb teas should always be consumed in moderation, because some of them are quite strong: for instance, the narcotic content of tansy tea should be used in small quantities only. It is advisable to brew herb teas in ceramic pots or jugs, and never in metal ones, because some herbs react unfavourably with a metal container.

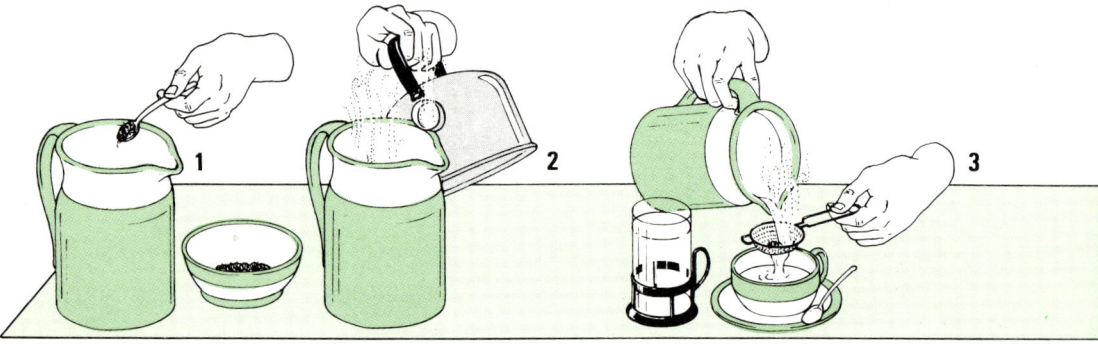

1 To make a tisane or herb tea from dried herb flowers or leaves, warm a china jug, and put into it a rounded teaspoonful of the herbs per cup. **2** Pour on the boiling water, and leave to stand for about 10 minutes; **3** then strain into tea cups.
4 Experiment with adding honey or lemon juice to taste, but *not* milk or sugar.

Remember one of the basic facts about herbs: the dried leaves or flowers are much stronger than the fresh ones. If making tea from fresh herbs, you will need to use larger amounts than those given above for the dried ones. Some teas are much better made with green leaves, eg lemon balm, lemon verbena, angelica.

An example of the difference between fresh and dried herbs is that when making bergamot tea with dried leaves you will find 1 teaspoonful per cup enough, but when using fresh leaves 3 teaspoonfuls per cup will be needed for a similar brew.

How to use herbs

Some leaf teas and their medicinal qualities
angelica, colds and catarrh
bergamot, sedative
hyssop, asthma
lemon balm, feverish colds
marjoram, loss of appetite
mints, headache and nausea
nettles, anaemia
rosemary, memory and eyes
sage, stimulates the brain
thyme, bronchitis

Not all herb teas are pleasant to the taste. Tansy tea is very bitter, and is usually taken in very small quantities for its medicinal qualities; it is mildly narcotic, and helpful against insomnia. White horehound makes another bitter brew, taken for colds and coughs. Both can be made more palatable with lemon juice and honey.

As well as making pure herb teas, you can experiment with blends. Two blends with alleged medicinal uses are lavender and rosemary (equal quantities), said to be beneficial for headaches, and camomile and lime flowers, which is useful in cases of chronic insomnia. Experiment with blends to find which one suits you.

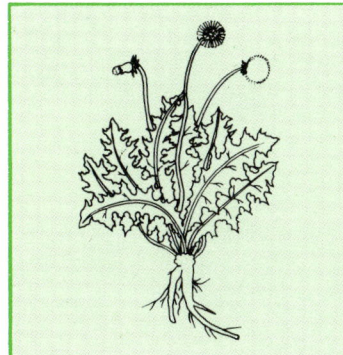

Dandelions are such a nuisance to the keen gardener that it is good to know that they have some uses too. Put 1 oz (28 gm) of fresh dandelion leaves into a jug and pour over them 1 pt (6 dl) of boiling water. Leave it to stand for about 10 minutes, then strain the liquid. Add honey as required.

Dandelion roots, fresh or dried, can be made into a pleasant drink sometimes used instead of coffee. Break the dandelion roots into small pieces, and bake on the middle shelf of a moderate oven for an hour or longer, until an even brown all over, turning them occasionally. Then grate the roots, and use as if it were coffee.

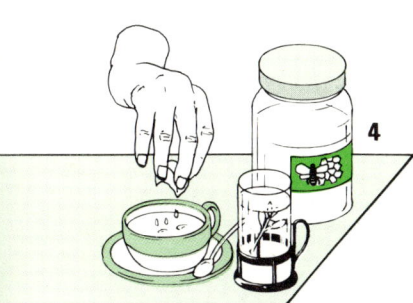

When serving a herb tea, be careful to strain it very thoroughly, so that no pieces of the leaves or flowers find their way into the tea cups. This is just as unpleasant as getting tea leaves in one's cup. It is only polite not to inflict herb teas on any visitor who shows some reluctance to experiment: remember, tastes differ.

Not all teas are hot drinks. They can be extremely refreshing taken cold on a warm summer day. Any kind of mint tea can be made in the usual way, straining it after it has been standing for 10 minutes. It can then be sweetened with honey if required, and chilled ready for use. Serve in small glasses with a sprig of fresh mint as decoration.

When herb seeds are used to make teas, they should be allowed longer to brew, usually about 20 minutes. The single exception to the method outlined above is rose-hip tea, which should be made with water that is almost, but not quite, boiling; boiling water would destroy the valuable Vitamin C content of the rose hips.

Wormwood tea, made in the same way as any other herb tea, is not even slightly tempting to drink, but it has other uses. If sprayed on the ground, it will discourage snails and slugs from attacking young plants. It will also discourage fleas if rubbed on the fur of cats or dogs.

fragrances

Home-made herbal preparations for use in the bathroom are far cheaper than commercially made ones, and often much more pleasing. They can be packed dry into muslin sachets or made up into a scented liquid, which can be used for many toilet purposes. You can make your own blends, and experiment with new ones; and as you can pick more herbs from the garden at any time, you can afford to be lavish with them! Dry sachets of herbs can also be used among linens, to keep them free from moths and to scent them sweetly.

Herb lotions can be used to wash one's face, or in the bath, or as a rinse after shampooing one's hair; they can also be used to scent the water in which clothes or linens are washed. To make a liquid preparation, take about half a cupful of your selected herbs from among the following: bergamot, lavender, lemon balm, lemon verbena, marjoram, mint, rosemary, sweet cicely, thyme. Pour on almost boiling water, and allow to stand for half an hour. Strain and pour the liquid into the hot water ready for use.
Needless to say, lavender is the great favourite for this (and many another) use. Equal parts of thyme and lavender make a pleasant brew with a difference. Men may feel that lavender is too scented, but the lemon herbs or mint may be to their taste. Try out various herbs and blends to find which suits your tastes. Some have special properties: camomile is good for ageing complexions, and marigold petals make a lotion that is beneficial against acne.

Sachets for the bath
Dried herbs are placed in small muslin bags with some rolled oats (which help to soften the water). The bags are then tied with thread. If a long thread is left, the bag may be hung from the hot tap. It is important to run the hot water first, to bring out the aroma of the herbs.

Sachets for linen
Perfumed linen was something our forefathers associated not with wealth or station, but with good housewifery. Indeed, the humble cottage was probably the origin of the herb-scented sachet tucked between sheets and pillow cases in the linen cupboard or the chest of drawers.
Lavender was the herb most often used among linen. But although the clean fragrance of lavender has a special quality, most of the sweet herbs can be used in this way.
Home-grown herbs in home-made sachets make a charming gift. Any tiny scraps of left-over fabric or ribbon can be used.

Myrrh
*And we are not told
whose gift was gold
Or whose was the gift of
Myrrh.*
Edmund Vance Cooke
(1866–1932) — *The Spirit of the Gift*

In mediaeval times, bugs and fleas flourished in the crowded and dirty conditions, and rue was highly valued because it kept them away. As these insects certainly spread diseases, rue was a valuable means of fighting infection. Many herbs also discourage flies, and these are still useful today: many cooks keep a vase with a few sprigs of fresh mint in the kitchen, and wormwood serves the same purpose. The herb sachets kept among linen in early times were intended not only to scent the sheets pleasantly, but also to discourage clothes moths: in addition dried wormwood or feverfew leaves were also used to protect household linens.

Rosemary hair rinse
This is both easy to make and very pleasant to use. Take a handful of young rosemary sprigs, just cover them in water (preferably rainwater) and simmer in a saucepan for about 10 minutes. Judge when the rinse is ready from the strength of the fragrance from the pan. Allow to cool, then strain.

Camomile lotion
This is a valuable rinse for fair hair, after washing. Use half a cupful of dried flowers to 4 cupfuls of water, and simmer for 10 minutes. Strain and leave to cool. Sage leaves make a good rinse for dark hair. Limeflowers and nettles are good for hair of any colour. Try making your own special blend.

Rue toilet vinegar
Bring 2 cups of water and 2 cups of white wine vinegar to the boil. Add 1 cupful of fresh rue and 1 cupful of sage, also 1 teaspoonful of powdered ginger. Bring back to the boil, then remove the pan from the stove and leave it to stand for about 12 hours. Strain, allow to cool, and then pour into bottles.

Scented toilet vinegar
Fill a jar half full with scented flower petals, then finish filling it with white wine vinegar. Stand in the sunshine for several days, and then strain off the liquid and bottle it. This makes a most refreshing toilet water, and a little of it used in washing water adds a faint flower scent to clothes.

To make lavender sachets, mix the ingredients in the following quantities:
1 cup of dried lavender flowers (usually removed from the stems, but this is optional), 1 cup of orris-root powder, ½ cup of dried rosemary leaves, and a few drops of oil of roses. Mix these well, and sew it into small thin sachets.

Lavender
An honest Ale-house where we shall find a cleanly room, Lavender in the Windows, and twenty Ballads stuck about the wall.
Izaak Walton (1593–1683) — *The Compleat Angler*

Chapter four

fragrant keepsakes

The scents of a garden at high summer are magical, and it is hardly surprising that for hundreds of years people have done their best to capture those scents and keep them for more than the few days that are the usual life of a flower. In ages when sanitation was not yet a fine art, such perfumes must have seemed even more desirable than they do now. Dried flowers were used in open bowls, in fabric sachets and in metal filigree containers, and their summer sweetness much have been welcome indeed.

Pot-pourri is rather a misnomer, because the name comes from the French *pot putrère*, which means a rotten pot; but it has now become the name for a mixture of the dried petals and leaves of scented flowers and herbs treated with spices. Most people think of pot-pourri as being made of flower petals, but scented leaves can also be used, eg geranium, lemon verbena, thyme. Include some brightly coloured petals too, if the mixture is to be used in open bowls. There are many recipes for making pot-pourri, and many fixatives are used: these are substances that keep the fragrance of the leaves and petals strong for many months. Perhaps the simplest to obtain is salt, but iodized salt is not suitable.

Pot-pourri can be of two kinds, wet or dry. Wet pot-pourri is used in a jar, and is usually covered over when not in use, the lid being removed when the room is occupied. Dry pot-pourri is used in sachets or pomanders. The method given below is for a wet pot-pourri.

petals
salt

Among the herbs and scented flowers commonly included in pot-pourri are: bay, borage, camomile, carnations, honeysuckle, jasmine, lavender, marigolds, marjoram, mignonette, pinks, rosemary, roses, stock, thyme (leaves), verbena, violets and wallflowers. For colour only, poppies, and delphiniums are useful.

To dry petals and herbs quickly, spread them out on a sheet of paper and cover them with a piece of net or other fine-meshed fabric. Fasten this down firmly all round, to prevent the petals from blowing away, and then use an electric hair-dryer on the petals. If not in a hurry, dry them in a warm place away from the light.

When the petals are fairly dry, mix them well. Put a layer into a large glass jar, then add a layer of salt (*not* iodized) half as thick. Repeat this process until the jar is full, pressing down firmly the whole time. You will find it takes more dried petals than you expect. Then keep the jar in a dark cool place for about 6 weeks.

How to use herbs

Pomanders are named from the French *pomme d'ambre*, meaning amber apple, because they were shaped like an apple, and ambergris was one of the ingredients used in making them. Various mixtures of herbs and spices were placed inside a spherical perforated case and these were hung from the wrist or attached to the girdle. Not only women carried pomanders: Henry V and Cardinal Wolsey are known to have used them too. They were believed to have medicinal powers against the plague, and in an age when washing was a minority pastime they were indeed a desirable luxury. Pomanders made of an orange stuck with cloves were slightly cheaper.

For making a pomander, you will need:
One Seville orange
Narrow tape
Pins
Cloves
Ribbon (usually velvet)
One paper bag
Cinnamon
Orris-root powder

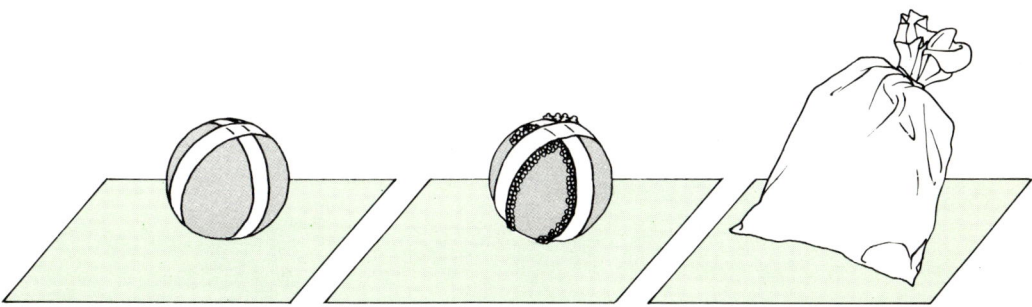

To make a pomander, mark an unblemished Seville orange into 4 equal sections with tape, fixing it with pins. Press cloves tightly together into the exposed orange skin. When all the areas of skin are covered with cloves, put the orange into a paper bag containing a mixture of equal parts of cinnamon and powdered orris root, and shake it up well to make the powder adhere. Keep the orange in the dark in a dry atmosphere for 3 weeks, either inside the powder bag or wrapped loosely in paper. Then remove the tape from around the pomander, and replace it with some decorative ribbon, making a hanging loop at the top. The clean and unusual perfume will last for many months, and if the pomander is hung in a wardrobe it is said to discourage moths too. Pomanders can also be made with an apple as the basis, or even a lemon, though this is more tricky to tie in ribbon afterwards.

Sweets

Various kinds of flowers can be eaten as part of a mixed salad, and whole borage and nasturtium flowers and the separated petals of marigolds are particularly valued for this, because they are decorative as well as tasty. But these are available only during the flowering season of the plants concerned. Several kinds of flowers and leaves can be crystallized and stored away in airtight containers for later use, to decorate the tops of cakes, puddings, and icecreams. Borage flowers can be crystallized whole, also sweet violets and rose petals. The leaves of mint are also often preserved in this way, but you can experiment with any plant that suits your taste. Angelica stems are also preserved by candying, and their bright green colour makes them decorative on top of cakes and trifle.

> *Fair is the rose, yet time will wither it;*
> *Fair the spring violet, but it quickly fades.*
> Theocritus (fl.285 BC)

Angelica
It is the stems of plants about three years old that are used for candying. Cut into sections 2 or 3 inches (4–7 cm) long, put them into boiling water, and boil till tender. Then peel them and cut the stems down their length. Return the pieces to the same water, and simmer them until they have become bright green (the addition of a cabbage leaf to the water will help to speed this process). Dry the pieces of angelica stem, weigh them carefully, and lay them in a pan with an equal weight of sugar. Leave them for 2 days, then heat to boil vigorously. Strain off the syrup. Take some more sugar and boil it to a syrup, then immerse the angelica stems in it for a few minutes, remove them, and spread them out to dry. The stems should now be crisp, tender and sugary. Store them in an airtight container until required.

How to use herbs 141

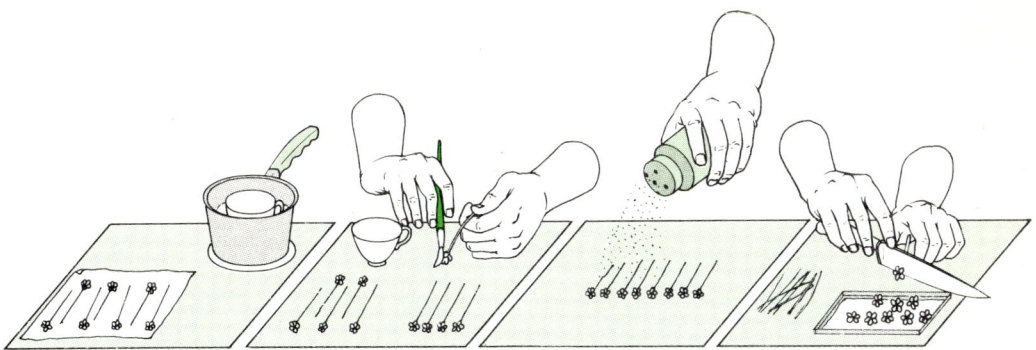

Crystallized violets
Choose perfect sweet violets and wash them gently. Place them well apart on a sheet of paper to dry naturally. Put the white of an egg into a cup, and warm it slightly in a saucepan of hot water. Then with a fine paint brush cover each flower with white of egg. Powder lightly with caster sugar until they are well covered, using the stems to turn the flowers over. Place them separately on sugared greaseproof paper laid on a baking sheet, cut off the stems, and keep in a warm dry place such as an airing cupboard until they are completely dry (at least 24 hours). Store in an airtight container until required.

Herbs in puddings
Herbs are mostly used with savoury dishes, but they can also add a pleasantly different taste to sweet ones. A single bay leaf will flavour a milk pudding very slightly. Mint is rather tasty with fruit salad or melon. And caraway seeds have been used for centuries to flavour bread and cakes.

Crystallized rose petals
Make sure that you gather flawless petals that are completely dry. Have ready 2 oz (56 gm) of gum arabic dissolved in ½ pt (3 dl) of water and allowed to cool. Spread out the petals on dishes and sprinkle them with gum arabic solution, then sprinkle with caster sugar and leave to dry for 24 hours.

Next, make a syrup from 1 lb (400 gm) of sugar in ½ pt (3 dl) of water, boiled to 250°F after the sugar has been dissolved. Colour with a little cochineal and allow to cool. Spread the sugared petals on shallow dishes, pour on the cooled syrup and leave undisturbed for 24 hours. Spread out the petals to dry on trays, and store in airtight container.

Herb sugars
Another use of herbs is to flavour sugar, which then gives a subtle taste to puddings and cakes. Put a broken vanilla pod, or a few leaves of rose geranium or mint, or a sprig or two of thyme in the middle of a jar of sugar (preferably caster sugar), and leave it to stand for a few weeks, giving an occasional stir.

Index

Bold numbers show main reference.

A
Absinthe, 55, 102
Agrimonia eupatoria, 26, 32
Agrimony, 16, 26, **32**
Alchemilla vulgaris, 96, 100
Alecost, 27, 85
Ale, horehound, 62
All-heal, 29
Allium sativum, 28
Allium schoenoprasum, 27, 34
Anethum graveolens, 27, 35
Angelica, 16, 17, 26, **36**, 60, 101, 134, 135, 140
Angelica archangelica, 26, 36
Angelica sylvestris, 36
Anise(ed), 16, 26, 38, 50, 51, **72**, 126, 132
Anthemis nobilis, 26, 37
Anthriscus cerefolium, 26, 38
Antiseptic, 66, 77, 85, 86
Applemint, 28, 64, 65
Arctium lappa, 96, 101
Artemisia absinthium, 96, 102
Artemisia dracunculus, 29, 39
Artemisia vulgaris, 96, 103
Asparagus, 101, 107
Asperula odorata, 104
Atropa belladonna, 96, 105

B
Balsam, 63
Balsam herb, 27
Basil, 12–13, 15, 16, 26, **69**, 77, 122, 123, 126, 128, 130, 131
Bath, herbs in the, 56, 59, 75, 120, 136
Bay, 11, 15, 16, 26, **57**, 122, 126, 128, 130, 131, 138, 141
Bee balm, 26, 66
Bees, 40, 59, 63, 66, 78, 85, 91
Beggar's buttons, 96
Belladonna, 96, 105
Bergamot, 12–13, 26, **66**, 134, 135, 136
Berries, 52, 56, 57, 79, 105
Betony, 96, 98, 99, **115**
Bishopswort, 96, 115
Bleeding, 100, 108, 117
Blood vine, 96
Boneset, 26, 27, 83
Borage, 11, 12–13, 26, **40**, 83, 122, 126, 138, 140
Borago officinalis, 26, 40
Bore tree, 28
Bouquet garni, 44, 57, 71, 86, 127
Boxberry, 29
Breads, 43, 47, 51, 60, 84, 127, 141
Bride's flowers, 68, 75
Bridewort, 96
Bronchitis, 79, 135
Bruisewort, 26, 27, 83
Burdock, 96, 98, 99, **101**
Burrage, 26
Burrs, 101
Bush basil, 69
Buttons, 29

C
Cakes and cake decoration, 40, 43, 47, 48, 84, 110, 140, 141
Calendula officinalis, 28, 42
Camomile, 12–13, 16, 17, 26, **37**, 79, 122, 132, 135, 136, 137, 138
Candying, 36, 60, 101, 140
Caraway, 16, 26, **43**, 49, 124, 126, 128, 132, 141
Carum carvi, 26, 43
Carum petroselinum crispum, 29, 44
Carum petroselinum fusiformis, 44
Catarrh, 72, 79, 85, 91, 135
Celery, 60, 72, 127
Chamomile, *see* Camomile
Chartreuse, 53, 63, 65, 67, 132
Cheeses, 43, 51, 81, 87, 128
Chervil, 12–13, 16, 26, **38**, 122, 126, 128, 130
Chickweed, 96, 98, 99, **113**
Chicory, 12–13, 16, 27, **45**
Chives, 12–13, 14, 16, 27, **34**, 122, 126, 130
Church steeples, 26, 32
Cichorium intybus, 27, 45
Clot-bur, 96
Cloves, 69, 139
Cloves of garlic, 33, 125
Cochlearia armoracia, 28, 46
Comfrey, 16, 26, 27, **83**
Common fennel, 50, 51
Common marjoram, 70
Common myrtle, 68
Common sorrel, 76
Common thyme, 31, 86
Common wormwood, 102
Compass plant, 29
Coriander, 16, 27, **47**
Coriandrum sativum, 27, 47
Corn poppy, 96
Corn salad, 16, 27, **89**
Costmary, 16, 27, **85**
Coughs, 62, 72, 91, 110
Court-bouillon, 129
Cow chervil, 29
Cowslip, 96, 99, **112**
Crocus sativus, 29, 48
Cuckoo-flowers, 101
Culpeper, Nicholas, 112, 113, 121
Cumin, 16, 27, **49**, 130
Cuminum cyminum, 27, 49

D
Dandelion, 96, 99, **116**, 133, 135
Deadly nightshade, 96, 98, 99, **105**, 109
Dead men's bells, 96
Devil's cherries, 96
Devil's herb, 96
Digitalis (drug), 106
Digitalis purpurea, 96, 106
Dill, 16, 19, 27, **35**, 51, 122, 126, 128, 130
Dried flowers, 59, 66, 79, 84, 92, 122–123, 134, 138
Dried herbs, 11, 35, 78, 81, 86, 106, 122–123
Drinks, flavouring of, 32, 40, 55, 63, 65, 67, 80
Dyes, 32, 48, 91

E
Eau de Cologne, 63, 75
Eggs, 38, 44, 128, 129
Elder, 16, 28, **79**, 122
Elderberry wine, 133
Elecampane, 16, 28, **55**
English lavender, 59
English sorrel, 76
Epilobium angustifolium, 96, 107
Evergreens, 15, 52, 53, 56, 57, 59, 68, 75, 77, 78, 86

F
Fairy cups, 96
Fairy thimbles, 96
Fennel, 12–13, 16, 26, 28, 35, 49, 50, **51**, 122, 126, 128, 129, 130
Fenugreek, 113
Feverfew, 137
Fines herbes, 34, 38, 44, 127
Finocchio, 16, 26, 28, **50**, 128
Fish, 38, 42, 46, 50, 51, 69, 72, 78, 86, 127, 128, 129, 130;
Florence fennel, 28, 50

Index

Foeniculum dulce, 28, 50
Foeniculum vulgare, 28, 50, 51
Foxglove, 96, 98, 99, **106**
French lavender, 59
French mustard, 39
French parsley, 44
French sorrel, 76
French tarragon, 39

G
Game, 56, 128, 130, 131
Garden mint, see Mint
Gardens, herb, 10–23
Garlic, 12–13, 16, 28, **33**, 126, 127, 128, 130
Garlic crusher, 125
Gaultheria procumbens, 29, 52
Gerard, John, 77, 103, 107, 114, 121
Germination, 14, 36, 44
Gifts, 127, 136–137, 138–139
Goose, 78, 103, 129
Gooseberries, 67
Green sauce, 29, 76
Grinding seeds, 123, 124
Growing herbs, 10–23; indoors, 14–15, 18–19, 22–23; outdoors, 12–13, 18–19, 23; wild, 98–99

H
Hair lotions, 75, 117
Hamamelis virginiana, 96, 108
Hamburg parsley, 44
Headaches, 75, 115, 135
Hemlock, 101, 121
Henbane, 96, 98, 99, **109**
Herb Louisa, 29
Herb of grace, 29, 71
Herb Peter, 96
Hips, rose, 74, 135
Hoarhound, 29
Hog's bean, 96
Horseheal, 55
Horseradish, 16, 28, **46**, 51, 126, 128, 129
Hyoscyamus niger, 96, 109
Hyssop, 12–13, 16, 28, **53**, 126, 128, 130, 132, 135
Hyssopus officinalis, 28, 53

I
Indoor herbs, 14–15, 18–23
Inula Helenium, 28, 55

J
Jackman's Blue, 77
Jacob's staff, 28
Juniper, 16, 28, **56**, 126, 131, 132
Juniperus communis, 28, 56
Jupiter's bean, 96

K
Kidney ailments, 44, 56, 106, 116
Kitchen herbs, 11, 12, 14, 15, 24–27, 124–131
Knitbone, 27, 83
Knotted marjoram, 28, 70

L
Lady's mantle, 96, 99, **100**, 123
Lamb's lettuce, 27, 89
Laurus nobilis, 26, 57
Lavandula spica, 28, 59
Lavandula stoechas, 28, 59
Lavandula vera, 28, 59
Lavender, 12–13, 16, 28, **58–59**, 135, 136, 137, 138
Lemon balm, 12–13, 17, 28, **63**, 132, 134, 135, 136
Lemon thyme, 86
Lemon verbena, 17, 21, 29, **61**, 134, 136, 138
Levisticum officinale, 28, 60
Levisticum scoticum, 60
Lion's foot, 96
Lippia citriodora, 29, 61
Liqueurs, 36, 43, 53, 63, 65, 67, 72, 86, 104, 132
Little dragon, 29
Lotions, 37, 51, 73, 79, 112, 117, 121, 136–137
Lovage, 17, 28, **60**, 123, 126, 128, 131
Love leaves, 96

M
Manzanilla, 26, 37, 132
Marigold, see Pot marigold
Marjoram, 12–13, 17, 28, **70–71**, 123, 126, 128, 131, 135, 136, 138
Marrubium vulgare, 29, 62
Marygold, 28
Meadowsweet, 96, 99, **114**
Meat dishes, 42, 50, 51, 53, 56, 60, 71, 78, 81, 86, 128, 131
Medicines, 47, 50, 104, 121, 139
Melissa officinalis, 28, 63
Mentha piperita, 28, 64
Mentha pulegium, 28, 64
Mentha rotundifolia, 28, 64
Mentha spicata, 28, 64
Mint, 11, 12–13, 14, 15, 17, 28, 53, 63, **64–65**, 66, 122, 123, 126, 128, 129, 130, 131, 132, 135, 136, 137, 140, 141
Mint sauce, 65
Mixed Herbs, 71
Monarda didyma, 26, 66
Morphine, 110
Mountain radish, 28
Mugwort, 96, 98, 99, 102, **103**

Mulching, 39
Mullein, 12–13, 17, 28, **91**
Myrrhis odorata, 29, 67
Myrtle, 17, 28, **68**
Myrtus communis, 28, 68

N
Narcotic content of herbs, 134, 135
Nasturtium, 12–13, 17, 29, **87**, 126, 128, 140
Nettles, 32, 63, 96, 98, 99, 101, 103, **117**, 135, 137

O
Ocimum basilicum, 26, 69
Oil cells, 35, 69
Oils, 43, 47, 50, 52, 53, 56, 57, 59, 65, 66, 74, 75, 86, 88, 110, 122, 124, 137
Ointments, 112, 113, 121
Onions, 33, 34, 35, 78, 129
Opium poppy, 96, 110
Oregano, 70
Origanum marjorana, 28, 70
Origanum onites, 28, 70
Origanum vulgare, 28, 70
Orris-root powder, 137, 139
Oswego tea, 26, 66
Our Lady's keys, 96

P
Papaver rhoeas, 96, 110
Papaver somniferum, 96, 110
Paralysio, 112
Parsley, 11, 12–13, 14, 17, 29, 38, **44**, 123, 126, 128, 129, 130, 131
Parsley mill, 125
Parts of herbs used, 26–29
Passerina, 96
Pennyroyal, 28, 64, 65
Pepper, 81, 87
Peppermint, 28, 64, 65
Perfumes, 26–29, 57, 59, 61, 74, 92, 104
Perseley, 29
Pestle and mortar, 124, 127
Petals, 42, 110, 112, 137, 138, 140, 141
Peter's staff, 28
Pickling, 35, 47, 56, 87, 120, 122
Pigweed, 29
Pimpinella anisum, 26, 72
Pipe tree, 28
Plague, 36, 139
Planning a herb garden, 10, 12–13, 16–17, 130–131
Plants, buying, 11, 16–17
Poisonous herbs, 96–97, 105, 106, 109, 117

Index

Pomanders, 26–29, 96–97, 120, 121, 138, 139
Poppies, 96, 99, **110**, 138
Popular names, 26–29, 31, 96–97
Pork, 78, 129
Portulaca oleracea, 29, 73
Portulaca sativa, 73
Potatoes, 44, 65, 127
Pot-bound plants, 22–23
Poterium sanguisorba, 29, 80
Pot marigold, 17, 28, **42**, 136, 138, 140
Pot marjoram, see Marjoram
Pot-pourri, 11, 121, 138; herbs used in, 26–29, 59, 61, 63, 68, 71, 74, 81, 96–97, 104, 138
Poultry, 60, 71, 128, 129
Priest's crown, 96
Primrose, 112
Primula veris, 96, 112
Puddings, 117, 140, 141
Purple rocket, 96
Purslane, 17, 29, **73**, 126

Q
Queen of the meadow, 96, 114

R
Radishes, 44
Red poppy, 96, 110
Red spider, 92
Repotting, 22–23
Roman laurel, 26
Root division, 16, 21
Rose, 13, 17, 29, 32, **74**, 138, 140, 141; see also Hips
Rosebay, 96, 107
Rose geranium, 141
Rosemary, 11, 12–13, 15, 17, 21, 29, **75**, 122, 123, 126, 128, 131, 135, 136, 137, 138
Rosmarinus officinalis, 29, 75
Rue, 17, 29, **77**, 137
Rumex (sp.), 29
Rumex acetosa, 76
Rumex scutatus, 76
Russian tarragon, 39
Ruta graveolens, 29, 77

S
Sachets, 11, 59, 61, 121, 136, 138
Saffron, 17, 29, 42, **48**, 126
Sage, 11, 12–13, 15, 17, 21, 29, **78**, 123, 126, 128, 129, 131, 135, 137
St John's plant, 96
Salad burnet, 12–13, 17, 29, **80**, 126

Salads, 38, 40, 42, 43, 44, 45, 50, 51, 60, 63, 65, 67, 73, 76, 77, 80, 87, 89, 92, 112, 113, 116, 126
Salvia officinalis, 29, 78
Sambucus nigra, 28, 79
Satureia (sp.), 29
Satureia hortensis, 81
Satureia montana, 81
Sauces, 38, 39, 44, 46, 56, 57, 63, 65, 69, 76, 86, 126, 127, 129
Savory, 15, 17, 29, **81**, 123, 126
Scabwort, 28, 55
Scottish lovage, 60
Sedatives, 88, 105, 109, 135
Seeds, 12, 16, 51, 124, 135; buying, 11; drying, 122–123; sowing, 16–17, 18–19; used, 26–29
Self-seeding, 11, 35, 38, 40, 91
Setwall, 29
Shepherd's needle, 29
Snapping hazelnut, 96, 108
Sorrel, 17, 29, **76**, 126
Soups, 35, 50, 51, 53, 57, 71, 73, 76, 80, 81, 86, 126, 127
Spearmint, 28, 64, 65, 132
Spices, 138, 139
Spike lavender, 59
Spinach, 40, 76, 113, 116, 117
Spiraea ulmaria, 96, 114
Spotted alder, 96
Stachys betonica, 96, 115
Starweed, 96
Stellaria media, 96, 113
Stews, 44, 53, 57, 71, 86, 126, 127, 131
Sticklewort, 26
Stickwort, 29
Stinging nettles, 96, 117
Strewing herbs, 77, 84, 85, 104, 114, 120
Stuffings, 71, 129
Succory, 27
Summer savory, 81
Sweet balm, 28, 122, 126, 128
Sweet basil, see Basil
Sweet cicely, 12–13, 17, 29, **67**, 126, 132, 136
Sweet fennel, 28
Sweet marjoram, 70
Sweet violet, see Violet
Sweet woodruff, 96
Swine's snout, 96
Symphytum officinale, 27, 83

T
Tanacetum balsamita, 27, 85
Tanacetum vulgare, 29, 84
Tansy, 12–13, 17, 29, **84**, 85, 134, 135
Taraxacum officinale, 96, 116

Tarragon, 12–13, 15, 17, 21, 29, **39**, 123, 126, 128, 131
Teaberry, 29
Teas, 32, 37, 40, 44, 51, 52, 53, 56, 60, 61, 65, 66, 75, 77, 79, 81, 88, 102, 103, 104, 107, 108, 115, 134–135
Thyme, 12–13, 15, 17, 21, 29, 31, **86**, 122, 123, 126, 128, 131, 135, 136, 138, 141
Thymol, 66, 86
Thymus (sp.), 29
Thymus citriodorus, 86
Thymus vulgaris, 86
Tisanes, see Teas
Toilet vinegars and waters, 121, 137
Transplanting, 18–19, 23
Tropaeolum majus, 29, 87

U
Urtica dioica, 96, 117
Urtica urens, 96, 117

V
Valerian, 17, 29, **88**
Valeriana officinalis, 29, 88
Valerianella olitoria, 27, 89
Vegetable plot, 11, 13
Vegetables, 45, 86, 101, 107, 113, 116, 117, 124
Verbascum thapsus, 28, 91
Verbena, see Lemon verbena
Vervain, 61
Veterinary medicine, 49, 55
Vinegars, 35, 39, 47, 56, 127, 137
Viola odorata, 29, 92
Violet, 17, 27, 29, **92**, 112, 138, 140, 141
Vitamins, 44, 74, 87, 92, 116, 135

W
Wallflowers, 138
White horehound, 17, 29, **62**, 135
White poppy, 96, 110
Wild sunflower, 28
Willow-herb, 96, 99, **107**
Window-boxes, 14–15
Wines, 36, 37, 73, 79, 104, 112, 114, 116, 132
Wines, equipment for making, 132–133
Wintergreen, 17, 29, **52**, 98
Winter savory, 81
Witches' gloves, 96
Witch hazel, 96, 98, 99, **108**
Woodruff, 96, 98, 99, **104**
Wormwood, 96, 98, 99, **102**, 103, 132, 135, 137